TRUE BOWLER ADJUSTMENTS

The enclosed information provides hundreds of tips for bowlers who wish to improve their knowledge of adjustments to combat lane conditions that are not favorable during play.

Bowlers make adjustments with the body. You can also adjust by selecting different bowling balls with surfaces that will interact with the lane. Lastly, bowlers make adjustments when they truly understand how lane conditions change during play. This understanding allows bowlers to track the ball with their eyes and play an area better suited for scoring.

What holds most bowlers back is the inability to keep building upon the knowledge and experience they already possess. For all bowlers there is a huge disadvantage when you lose the ability to use the same bowling language or "lingo" as those who advance and find great success. Hearing that the lanes are "tight" means they are in fact "oily" so you may have to play a tight line and not have an area like most house shots.

Learn the difference between your A-Game and your B-Game. Continue to be a student of the game and educate yourself!

My sincere thanks goes out to the proshop staffers, weekly house bowlers, amateurs, professional bowlers and to Mr. Andy Clark (RIP) of Cactus Bowl, Tucson, Az .

Over the last 10 years, you have allowed me to sit, listen to your conversations, and observe your practice sessions like a fly on the wall.

The most enjoyable exchanges will always be the conversations in which no words were spoken, yet you clearly translated to me what you were doing with each delivery, good or bad.

-TrueBowler

Big
Concepts **O**

Thank you for purchasing True Bowler Adjustments.
A general table of contents has been provided.

Thank you for purchasing True Bowler Adjustments.
You have just invested in your future when it comes to bowling
awareness on the lanes. Let us get started!

TRUE BOWLER ADJUSTMENTS

Mastering the Game – <u>**Consistency**</u> is a bowler's watchword. **Consistency** with your **release**. **Consistency** with **balance at the line**. **Consistency** at **targeting**. Lastly, **consistency** with **where you land the ball on the lanes**. These are in order of your highest priorities to master.

(5 Points to consider as you Advance your level of play)

1- **For All Bowlers -** <u>**Ball fit and ball weight.**</u> **Ball weight** is important in manipulating the distance at which you will release the ball either closer to you, or further out on the lane away from you during play. **You cannot do this with poor ball fit or a ball that is too heavy.**

2- **For All Bowlers -** <u>**Release**</u> – Getting the ball off your hand with lift/spin can come from **four** areas of the hand: both lateral sides of the hand, the mid-palm, and lift towards the thumb. When you find <u>your **consistency of release,** ball drillers can properly layout various reactions on bowling balls using your Positive Axis Point (PAP).</u>

3- **For Established Bowlers -** <u>**Balance at the line**</u> - Consistency to the line without tilting over too much, **(falling off your shot)** at release will allow a bowler to observe where the ball lands on the lane, as well as the ability to watch **the ball's reaction** is as it travels down lane.

4- **For Advanced Bowlers -** <u>**Ball layout**</u>- Layouts can provide a stable roll to your ball or delay its hooking ability and violent reaction point early or later down lane to match up with the existing lane conditions.

5- **Tournament Bowler**s - Understand <u>**lane conditions and the length of the oil patterns**</u> - Finding out the **length of the oil patterns** and investigating **oil volumes across the lane**, may help you to select an area to play. Selecting **the proper grit cover** to clear the heads and **create the proper reaction down lane is crucial!** Learn to select the proper bowling ball based on prior experience. Make notes of layouts to use for maximum scoring potential. Gain experience and **remember** your lane play. **Consistent performance is the key.**

True Bowler Adjustments is like sitting down at a buffet. You will see many things you will want to try. However, not everything listed is for everybody. Some adjustments may work for you. Others may not.

Beginner to Established bowler Adjustments 130 – 150 average

The Body

Your body - You can move up, back, to the left, and to the right on the lanes. <u>You do not have to stand in a particular spot.</u> Your body can lean back on your back foot to slow your steps, or you can lean forward slightly onto your lead off foot to speed up when your feet are separated a little. Much like a runner's position on the starting line.

Head - Tilt forward a bit with balance. Eyeball **two targets** as you bring your head down smoothly, without bouncing in your delivery. Try not to bring your head past the knee or the toe of your slide foot. Two targets in bowling are better than having just one.

EYES - They look closer to you on the lane, allowing you to release earlier at a target. Balance and timing will be optimum. Looking further down the lane, will help to project the ball further allowing for increase ball travel. It will also aid in acquiring loft that can sometimes bring the ball into the pins earlier. **Established and Advanced bowlers know that the most important weapons in your arsenal are your eyes! They aid in reading the ball's reaction down lane.**

Targeting with your eyes – Bowlers like big targets, however bigger targets are usually so far away. Those who deliver the ball with **a spin release** most of the time, are looking farther down lane to the break point at release. Often bowlers will never move their eyes from that point. This requires a lot of hand eye coordination.

Eye Dominance: Bowlers who are right handed yet left eye dominant may have difficulties with delivery. You must compensate so that you do not deliver the ball **short of your targets.** Same for right eye dominant left handed bowlers. Most people will check eye dominance by looking through a 1 to 2 inch circle, made with the hands held about 1 foot in front of the face. While focusing on a target on the wall at least 10 to 20 feet away, alternate closing the left eye then, the right eye. The eye **you prefer** to have open, to see through the hole, **is your dominant eye.** Once you find out you are one of the many who may have an opposite eye domination issue, aligning your forearm for proper ball projection may become key to consistent scoring. **(Simple check)** One of the biggest clues to figure this out is aligning your forearm down lane to a pin or range finder. If when you do this, you may not realize you are aligning to a pin to the left of where you are aiming. A friend standing behind you may check this, or most appropriate, **a certified coach**. Coaches will look at your alignment and projection angle to a pin or range finders on the lanes. **Coaches have different methods** for correcting opposite eye dominance issues.

    Eyes on the lanes: Take a moment to look at the lanes closely from now on. Each lane will have its own **"foot print"** so to say. Those small patches or dark or light spots only six to 8 inches apart **will line you up to another target down lane, making you very accurate.** Crossing these **"spots"** on the lane, **light or dark colored** along with a dot or an arrow, can also help you play angles to the backend. **End-over-end release bowlers and many others** will roll over these landmarks consistently to get to the headpin, or to convert spare shots. **Sometimes the biggest targets are the small ones just at the end of your swing!**

SHOULDERS - Turn your shoulders to your target as you move across the approach. Always face your target truly, as well as walking directly to your target.

YOUR BOWLING "SHOULDER" – Once you find the release you like off of your hand, **you must next master how and when to throw with the upper arm turned to the outside.** *(Open your "SHOULDER" UP, and not your SHOULDERS)* at release. **When the upper arm is turned inside you will be (CLOSED SHOULDERED) at release.** Each rotational aspect of the upper arm has its advantages and disadvantages during play. One **advantage** of *(Opening your shoulder)*, or rotating the **upper arm to the outside, elbow into the body**, is increased ease of **ball tilt** if desired as well as **decreased axis of rotation** to create more length of the ball down lane. This helps to promote storing more energy at the pocket. One **disadvantage of rotating the upper arm inward** would be limiting the clockwise positioning of the hand (right handed bowlers), and **creating increased side roll** that can often be undesirable on dry conditions which may often cause the ball to dive through the headpin or go Brooklyn on short patterns. **Inside rotation of the upper arm may cause you to grab the ball** at the bottom of the swing.

Often times the outward rotation of the upper arm will promote a cleaner lift and roll off the hand and fingertips. This rotation will provide a stable wrist position. Often the balance and support of the ball will be transferred to the thumb side of the hand for the inside turn of the upper arm.

Alternatively, **the balance and support of the ball transfers to the pinky side of the hand** and arm for the outside rotation of the upper arm. Overall, there is a time and place for upper arm adjustments along with the most appropriate hand position.

ARMS – Know your ball height position. <u>**This is a key to repeating your shots!**</u> If you want the ball to go longer, raise the ball slightly in your beginning stance. Push away directly at your first target in-line with your second target down lane. Lowering the bowling ball at the beginning of your starting position and releasing it from a lower projection point will usually get the ball to finish stronger. Lowering the ball also will allow you to move faster to the foul line - <u>if needed.</u> It is better to lower the ball when attempting to use loft on the ball to keep it on-line to your target.

ELBOWS - Cup of the elbow needs to face down lane to achieve a free arm swing. This way you do not muscle the ball. **Exercise:** Extend your arm out in front of you with the palm of your hand to the floor. You will see the back of your hand to the ceiling; your wrist is parallel to the floor. Your elbow cup **(elbow joint)** will generally be at 45 degrees to the floor. Now, ever so slowly, turn your wrist and hand until you thumb is pointing up toward the ceiling. Now look at your elbow. Chances are your elbow is still at a 45-degree angle to the floor. **This shows you can keep the elbow still, rotating only the hand and wrist at release often just a ¼ turn.**

Most often, when a bowler is doing well at one point, and then just seemingly falls apart and unable to score, the cup of the elbow is no longer facing the pin at release. They have **"chicken winged" or bent the elbow,** out to the 45-degree turn of the elbow and lost ball reaction. Ball is not finishing at the pocket. This coupled with late timing can leave a bowler lost and confused. **Always check your timing first!** Then see if you are keeping the elbow in the correct position. Remember, sometimes delivering the ball **closed shouldered**, can make the ball dive through the middle **depending on your release**.

TrueBowler realizes you will see people throwing back up balls all the time. The over rotation (turning) of the elbow and upper arm, under, into and away from the body is noted most often with back up bowlers. The span could be part of the problem also. **Those who throw back up balls and wish to change to a standard release definitely need to seek out a coach who can guide them to a successful release.** This way, tried and true adjustments can be used to score higher. Those who are successful with backup balls are very few in number. Do not turn the elbow and arm, just wrist and the hand. <u>**However**</u>, if you have **a good backup ball release**, to me that would definitely qualify as your **D - Game**!!! Two-handed bowling would be your **E - Game! If you think about it, no matter which release you use, you will spin the ball or end-over-end it probably.**

   MENTAL GAME!!! - "Observing others" who score well, and watching the elbow along with its path towards the pins, will help you focus on repeating shots. Still most importantly you always have to watch, are they spinning the ball, are they end-over-end releasing the ball or are they lofting the ball out a little, or are they setting the ball down early.

   Wrist - The wrist is a freely movable joint, **to score well you have to firm it up in a good position (make the wrist stiff), and use that firm/stiff position in different variations** to deliver good shots. <u>**Wrist supports**</u> can definitely help with increased ball reaction. Position the wrist **vertically** to the floor, **horizontal or flat to the floor,** or **obliqued** to the floor at delivery.

 Wrist Positioning

VERTICAL   HORIZONTAL   OBLIQUED

As taught to me, it often takes the body **1500 times** to learn a new muscle movement. **Practice spinning the ball "at your ankle" to develop good rotational spin and revolutions on the ball.** Do not let the wrist collapse back toward the body and go around the bottom of the ball while in the forward swing, you may suffer from recurring loss of speed on the ball.

Cupping the wrist is an adjustment. Bowlers will cup the wrist to get a reaction that is different. This cupping is only going to be one to two inches from their normal grip of neutral or slightly flexed wrist. Cupping the wrist will often increase the revolutions on the ball. Increasing skid just a bit at times but often increasing traction on the backend. This depends on how early or how late the **"roll"** phase of the ball is down lane, and the length of the oil pattern. It is ok to try to cup the ball just a little, but if it does not give you a definite change in reaction, do not waste precious frames trying it. That is what practice time should be used for.

Breaking the wrist downward often reduces the number of revolutions on the ball allowing the ball to get traction earlier on the lanes to bring the ball in sooner if you are overthrowing the breakpoint. Often you will use this adjustment **when leaving 10 pins.** End-over-end bowlers or **forward rolling** players may benefit the most from this adjustment. Breaking the wrist downward is a great training position for those who aspire to reduce their sidespin on the ball to a more forward spin. At times, spinning the ball will cause it to go too long, or skid too far to the outside near or into the channel or gutter on the lanes. Forward rolling ball in the beginning of the game, on fresh oil, will often keep the ball well within the area of play.

Delivering the Ball **"Always, have at least two ways to release the ball."**

(The 8 P's) Thanks Kevin Holder RT(R) !!!!

Prior, proper, planning, prevents, piss poor, performance Playa!

When the end-over-end is not working, perhaps spinning the ball at release may work. Not having two ways to release the ball is not an option ...generally speaking. The lanes do not care that you can only throw the ball one way! Practice, practice, practice at least two releases and see what the difference is between them.

Axis Rotation: Zero degrees, 45 degrees and 90-degree release to the lane.

Below is an image illustrating releasing the ball straight down lane to the pins: **Zero rotation** or end-over-end release will go straighter down the lane. With this release, **the bowler creates hook on the ball by varying the ball axis rotation and the ball axis tilt.** Again, this release position utilizes a flat wrist position to the floor.

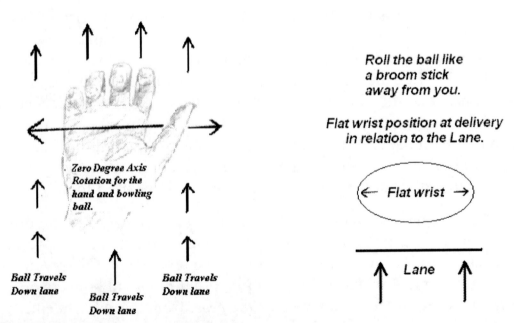

Roll the ball like a broom stick away from you.

Flat wrist position at delivery in relation to the Lane.

Flat wrist

Lane

Zero Degree Axis Rotation for the hand and bowling ball.

Ball Travels Down lane

Ball Travels Down lane

Ball Travels Down lane

Bowling ball is released onto the lane from this hand position. This zero degree hand position has the maximum amount of skid and least amount of hook potential traveling down lane. This is often termed the straight ball release.

Axis Rotation: 45 degrees release to the lane. Below is an image illustrating releasing the ball straight down lane to the pins: **45-degree rotation** with moderate side roll, down the lane.

From this position, you can spin the ball at release, or flip it end-over-end at a 45-degree angle to your target on the lane. Wrist position can vary from a flat wrist position, to an obliqued (unstable) wrist position at release, which is illustrated on the next page.

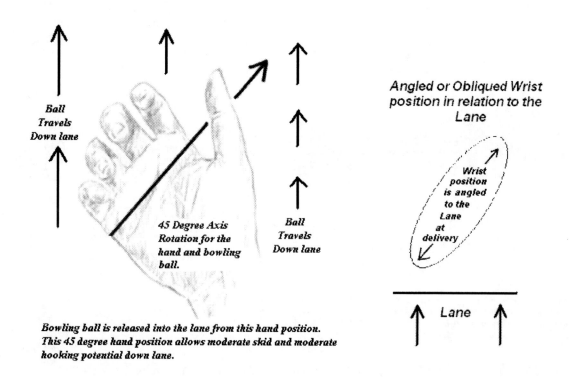

Bowling ball is released into the lane from this hand position. This 45 degree hand position allows moderate skid and moderate hooking potential down lane.

Axis Rotation: 90-degree release to the lane.

On the next page, is an image illustrating releasing the ball straight down lane to the pins: **90-degree rotation** or maximum side rotation down the lane. With this release towards your target, the ball spins from the 3 o'clock position from the side of the ball while traveling towards your target. (9 o'clock for lefties) **the wrist position is often vertical to the floor at release.**

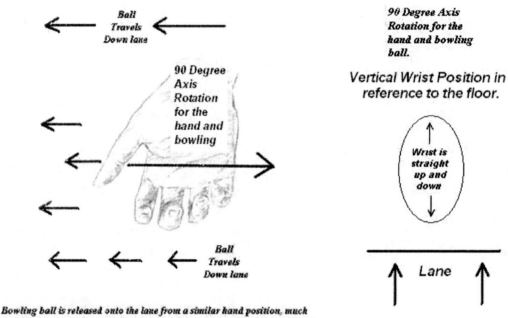

Bowling ball is released onto the lane from a similar hand position, much like that of holding a suitcase handle beside your body. This 90 hand position allows moderate skid on the front end or heads and the most violent hook potential for the ball on the backend.

All hand release positions (axis rotation or axis tilt) can be varied by the bowler however; **the key to good scoring is to "remember" your hand position and release angle to the lane during play."**

You could be using very different axis rotations from lane to lane in order to score well, depending on the lane condition.

<u>**THE SUPPORT HAND:**</u> Use the hand that you do not throw the ball with as a guide, to place the ball <u>at the same height</u> in your beginning stance every time. Coaches prefer that you support the ball through the push away with the support hand from **underneath** or from **the side.**

Others will tell you **to place your support hand to the side, front, top, or bottom of the ball** so that you can **"see"** <u>how high you are holding the ball</u>

on each delivery. If the ball "needs" to be lowered, your hand will come to the **side, front,** or **under** the ball for support. Again, you will easily be able to note the ball height. You have to see in practice if this makes you better at repeating your shots.

"Axis Rotation control" – With your non-ball hand on the side of the ball, use this **support hand** to help adjust your axis rotation front to back (zero to 90 degrees) **as well as up and down axis tilt! Especially when using the forward roll otherwise known as the End-over-End release. Do not allow the non-ball hand be lazy!** Get it into the game! You can repeat shots if you set the ball up correctly. Use the non-ball hand to set up your ball.

Find **a coach that can** show you how to make these types of adjustments, up and down, front to back. This will help control your **"roll"** on the backend!

Support hand or non-ball hand - For good balance, you can also try keeping the thumb down on the non-bowling hand. This is accomplished after it releases the ball and throughout the rest of the delivery. This will allow the support hand to swing back more naturally if needed.

THE BOWLING HAND can fit the ball in several ways allowing you to **feel** the weight of the ball on different parts of your hand:
(1) from the middle finger and across the palm to the thumb;
(2) from the ring finger across the palm to the thumb with weight of the ball at the base of the ring finger and middle finger;
(3) the weight of the ball can be balanced from the ring finger, back to the base of the index finger and the thumb with the primary **feel** of the ball at the base of the index finger where the ball rotates at the release / pivot point.

The most interesting thing about adjusting with your hand and "the feel" that comes with getting the ball to react to the lane is that you must try to verbalize how you release the ball into the lane.

To the point - **Do you spin the ball** into the lane like a top? Do you flip the ball into the lane like throwing a football underhanded and counter clockwise **using sidespin?** Or, do you use the **end-over-end for forward roll on the ball?** Lastly, do you come from the back of the ball and to the side of it, **spinning, rotating and lifting** the ball at release? As a coach, I want you to learn to do as many releases as you can, as proficiently as you can!

Release – Your - A, B, and C - Games

Your A-Game: Let there be no doubt that your A-Game is **the delivery that you are most consistent at repeating.** For some bowlers it may be the spinning release, for others it may be their end-over-end release and for the elite few, it may be a combination of spin, **forward roll, lift and spin.** Regardless, your A-Game is **the release you can repeat consistently with no problems.**

So what is your A-Game?
"End-over-end release, Spinning release, or combination spin, forward roll, lift and spin release, full roller release, back-up ball release, 90 degree side roll release or for the international players the helicopter release?"

Your B-Game: This is your **second release that you are just as comfortable delivering**. Your B-Game release is **the release you practice and practice until you are just as confident with it** as you are your A-Game release. If you spin the ball your B-Game is End-over-end or some other kind of release you are very good at repeating.

Your C-Game: This is **a variation of the combination of the two releases.** When lane conditions are not favorable, you may have to added or subtract ball tilt, or axis rotation to affect ball travel, or roll, for the lane condition.

When you practice, first you should deliver your A-Game release from your normal delivery position and then try your B-Game release from your normal delivery position on the approach. This will allow you to see how the bowling ball reacts down lane through the area your have chosen with respect to each release.

Ball Swing / Ball Travel – Delivering Straight and Delivering a Curve

I am deliberately placing the following illustrations here to help bowlers understand how "wrist position" and hand position, plays a role in **"where"** and **"how"** your bowling ball travels on the lane.   You will see charts in the pro shops that depict **how** your ball may be traveling down the lane. Often it shows **where it travels,** like a big curve, a slight curve from the outside part of the lane or it shows a straight shot down and in. It will also show approximately the length of the oil pattern that **the ball you are looking at** will travel based on a certain type of release shown on the chart.

Pro Shop Charts

Find the average oil pattern for "your house" in terms of oil length. It will typically be represented in foot measurements or wording such as "Light or Short Oil," "Medium Oil," or "Heavy or Long Oil."

Light oil 25 to 35 feet. Medium oil, 35 to 40 feet. Heavy or Long oil, 43 to 45 feet.

" The typical house shot is normally 37 to 40 feet of oil. "

If you have the Four Range Finder Markers on the newer synthetic lanes, the beginning of the second set of Range Finder Markers is approximately 40 feet. The oil line in the house I bowl in stops about a foot in front of the range finder markers giving me a 39-foot shot, which I love! I can be so slow some days. Find out if your house oils to 37 ft. or even down to 40 ft! Lucky devils!

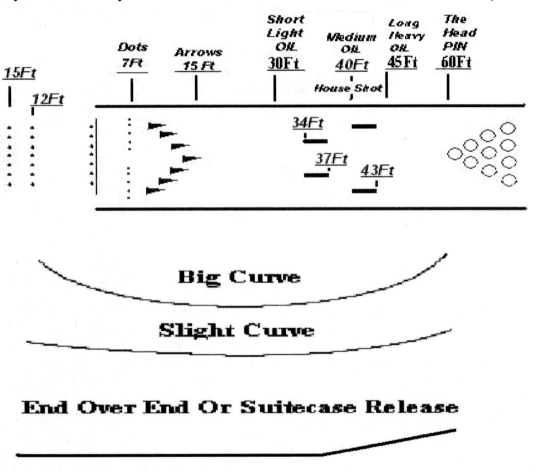

The above ball paths to the pins can be duplicated with the bowling balls in the pro shops. This is based on your **type of release, wrist and hand position,** and ball travel **per lane condition illustrated on the chart.**

If your ball travel looks like the Big Curve chart above, then any bowling ball you are interested in buying needs to have the Big Curve on the chart, so the pro shop can drill it for you. Make sure to tell them you throw a big curve, or have them come out and watch you deliver a few shots.

If you deliver your ball and the ball travel looks like the **End-Over-End** or **Suitcase Release** picture, **this is throwing the ball straight down the lanes.** You should select a ball that can be drilled with a layout that will give you that type of ball travel **because your release is** such that you deliver the End-over-End, or a suitcase style of delivery **straight down the lane.**

Un-stable and Stable Wrist Positions

Un-Stable Wrist Position

The first illustration shows how the 45-degree position of the wrist uses up the front part of the lane. **Bowlers often complain about "not being able to hit their target" because of this wrist position. They might be unknowing incorporating this wrist position into their delivery.**

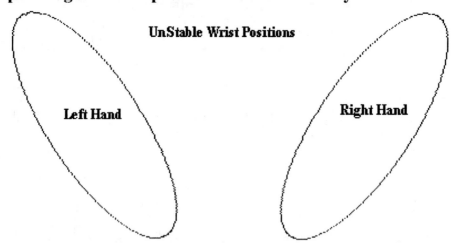

Unstable wrist position at release. 45 degrees to the lane often will cause the delivery to spin inside or outside of the target. Highly skilled players and players who are quite deliberate with their wrist positioning find success with this delivery.
This wrist position with a spinning release will track excessively to the outside. The end-over-end release will always be straighter and more of a consistent read to the back end as long as you come up the back of the ball during release and not spin the release to the outside.

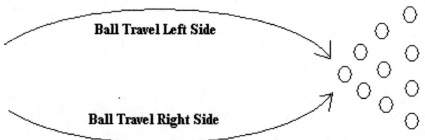

Often when a player complains about not hitting their target, they are delivering a combination release. The player starts out holding the ball end-over-end to release it to the lanes, yet they end up spinning the ball off their hand **where the fingers exit the side of the bowling ball at release.** This spin, causes the ball to move right of target to the outside for bowlers, especially in high or fresh oil on the front end of the lanes, the area just after the foul line. **Spin the ball out of dryer heads to the backend, not high oil.**

Stable Wrist Positions

With a stable wrist position, you are more consistent with your delivery. Revs, leverage and balance at the line can be easier to apply on the approach. Missing front-end targets are often minimized.

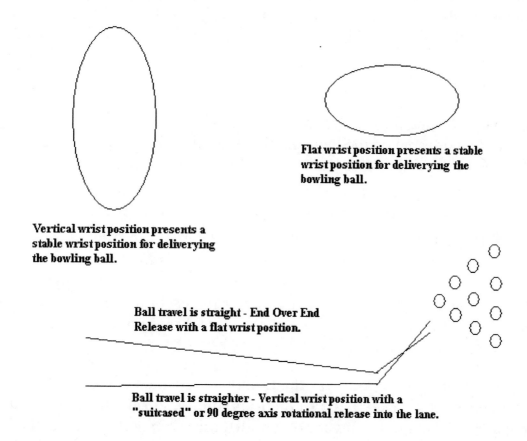

Flat wrist position presents a stable wrist position for delivering the bowling ball.

Vertical wrist position presents a stable wrist position for delivering the bowling ball.

Ball travel is straight - End Over End Release with a flat wrist position.

Ball travel is straighter - Vertical wrist position with a "suitcased" or 90 degree axis rotational release into the lane.

Swing Management – Are you getting to the head pin in good shape or are you coming in high leaving spare shots? Should the ball come in too high, many high level players use **the push away as an adjustment** to extend the distance of ball travel. Also, when they leave the first corner pins, or you leave the 5 - 7 split or the 5 pin spare. Players **create leverage, slow their spin, or create more traction at the backend by swinging slower with the ball.** Leaves like the 5 – 7, the 5 or the 10 pin, is a great indicator that your ball **is rolling out too far away from the head pin or worst, skidding into**

or pass the headpin. **Knowing how your arm swing will finish is also part of swing management**. Will it finish **12 o'clock above your head** or out to **the 1 o'clock position.**

Fingers - Spreading the index finger will often result in the shot going longer. The amount of distance you spread the finger out often times in relation to the amount of ball tilt you plan to release into the lane. If you spread your index finger wide, you will find you can literally parallel your two middle fingers to the floor during your back swing with your hand on the outside of the ball. Also, as you bring the index finger back into your hand, the wrist will relax and come back more in-line with arm. This will allow you to use a more controlled release. When releasing a straight ball spreading the index finger and the pinky will flatten the shot out. Giving you **end-over-end roll,** or a straighter ball when releasing with your hand directly behind the ball from the 6 o'clock position; the 5 o'clock position; or from the 3 o'clock position, where you start with your hand under, or to the side of the ball.

Ring finger- Placing pressure on the pad of the ring finger will often provide a little more spin on the ball(spinning release) and forward travel on the ball(end-over-end release) however, balance may be affected.

Relying on the ring finger to push the shot further to the right has been an old trick of bowlers for years. Especially if you are going Brooklyn on the head pin, or a little bit high on the headpin and leaving the 4pin.

Another example of adjusting with the ring finger is using it to convert the 10 pin. The right-handed bowler will use the ring finger to direct the shot at the 10 pin. (**Right handed** = The shorter finger for the higher numbered pin) (**Left handed**= The shorter finger for the shorter numbered pin to pick up the 7 PIN)

Middle finger- its connection with the thumb and rotation of the ball cannot be understated. **They need to be in harmony.** For the times you apply pressure to the middle finger giving it **lift and spin** at the release, the ball will most often turn back sharply (side turn) when done correctly giving the ball finish at the pocket to **kick out the 5 pin and the 10 pin. Applying pressure to the middle finger provides for an earlier entry into the pocket.** Especially, when you are under the ball more. This can also cause the ball to roll out early if conditions are too dry.

The most interesting thing about using the **middle finger** concerning adjustments is the ability to be deadly accurate when picking up pins to the left side of the lanes. Most players (right handed) concentrate more energy on the **middle finger and just a little pressure on the ring finger, when attempting spares to the left.** This adjustment keeps most players from dumping the ball off the ring finger when attempting to pick up left sided spare shots. (**Right handed** = Longest finger at the lower numbered corner pin 7 PIN) (**Left handed** = Longest finger at the highest numbered corner pin 10 PIN) The middle finger pitches can control axis rotation somewhat. Pitching to zero or to the right will allow you to axis rotate less than 45 degrees easier. Pitching to the left will increase rotation above 45 degrees.

Pinky tuck - The pinky tuck is often used by those who want to add a little "pepper" to the turning of the ball on the lane. Tucking the pinky, allows for extra ball tilt at release, or more controlled spin at release. It takes lots of practice. Some players even push the ball with the tucked pinky. You will see a callus build up on the joint. **(Often the pinky is too long to do this.)** This pinky tuck seemingly adds more torque, or turn at the bottom of the swing. Torque or turn of the ball far left of 30 is often useful along with a little loft! **This shot can be described as that action of the ball on the lane when it is revolving very fast, but not moving forward extremely fast.** Players who throw the "big wheeling" curve on the lanes will frequently use the pinky tuck. (As long as the **pinky is short enough** to do this without recurring injury!). Most bowlers place only the nail of the pinky on the ball.

Fingers "Pinky"- Pinkies often get hurt at the tip when they are not split out from the ring finger. **(Mostly, End-over-End bowlers with "longer" pinkies.)** Separating the pinky out from the hand often times puts the ball in control of the other four fingers. For maximum control of the ball the bowler feels every aspect of the ball, turn, lift, rotation, and spin are often greatly reduced. So much so, to the point the bowler is stiff or jerky at release. However, because of the slowness and all things considered this comes as no shock that on a long oil pattern this release serves a purpose to allow for decrease speed and deliberate control to the pins. Splitting the pinky out most often is used to decrease forward axis rotation, allowing for a **straighter ball release** with the **hand behind the ball**. This can give longer skid through the front end. Spare shooting and delivering the ball up the 5 board is a useful strategy to practice when splitting the pinky out and staying behind the ball. Pinky in, often spins the ball. It takes a little practice, but you can provide more forward momentum, and lift to the ball **with the pinky finger** and **the index finger** supporting the ball through the release.

Finger pads "Middle and Ring finger pads"- Provide lift and **spin** to the ball when it needs to clear heads or otherwise to assist in shot making. You should **feel** the ball come off the pads of your fingers last upon release. Those who spin and rotate on the release will often comment that **they do not feel** the ball off the pads of their fingers. Those who crank the ball will comment that the tips and pads of there fingers sometimes have a "burning" sensation on them. The different between the two can be simplified by the follow explanation hopefully: **"Imagine there is no oil on the lanes and you are bowling on wood lanes like back in the old days.** If you were trained to bowl with your **middle and ring fingers curled** in the ball through the entire swing through the release (especially during a forward end-over-end release) you saw the ball do an amazing thing, it would "hook" off the lanes. The fingers inside the ball remained stiff and locked to the back of the walls the finger holes in the curled position. Not necessarily gripping or squeezing the ball, just firm through the back swing and release.

"Roll the ball"

If your ball was hooking too much, a coach had to find a way to help your ball go longer down the lanes. If you ever heard the term **"Roll the ball"** this means that you did not release the ball into the lanes with your fingers curled to the back walls of the grip, thus you would not be providing lift and spin to the shot. Only lift! Often times when someone just **"rolls the ball"**; they get very little revs at the back end. The ball **"rolls"** down the lane skidding more. It will go very long because you are not "grabbing the ball." You are just pushing the ball off your hand and finger joints, down the lane. In certain cases such as drier lanes, you may need this adjustment get farther down lane. It takes practice to master this adjustment.

Many times bowlers may **"roll the ball"** or **push the ball off their finger joints** inconsistently causing the ball to either push pass the target area, …or they actually **"hit up"** on the ball. Going from (a relaxed finger position which is straighter towards the floor) to a curled position at the end of the swing. This causes them to **"hit up"** on the pads of their fingers to the back of the finger holes, trying to get the ball to rev up or spin more so that it will finish better at the pins. On a dryer lane would truly be the time to eject the ball off the finger joints if you did not have a higher surfaced ball in your bag. Dirt or **black lane tar** (as I call it!) inside the finger holes denotes loss of contact in the finger holes especially if it is where the finger pads rest.

Curling the finger tips

One of the toughest things in bowling is learning to deliver the ball **with your fingers curled to the back of the fingertip grips** through release. If your ball is properly fitted, **then the pads of your fingers will sit on the back of the finger holes at all times.** When done properly you learn **to throw through the ball** and provide **lift and "spin"** to the ball when it travels down lane. Eventually **the ball will loose speed** just pass mid lane where the "hamsters" or **weight blocks inside the ball** can take over, rev up, and start making the run to the pins and crush the 5-pin! **Although this is a short paragraph, this curling of the fingers is extremely important in bowling. When to curl the fingers and when not to curl the fingers is something that can be overlooked by coaches. Ball fit is crucial to getting the ball to sit properly on the pads of the fingers.**
Inserts or finger holes should not be too lose, or too snug. Sometimes **a smaller size insert** will solve the problem of loss of contact, or **using away pitch** may solve this issue.

Thumbs and Thumbholes - When drilling thumbholes, not much left to right pitch, forward or reverse pitch is used. Changing the angle of the thumb in the ball (**the pitch**) can help you hold onto the ball longer (without squeezing). It will not allow the ball to come off your hand too soon. Proper fit will allow for a consistent delivery towards the pins. **This part requires the experts at the pro shops to look at things for you.** Monitor your release to see if the ball is falling off your hand, or if the ball is hanging up on your thumb, or worst yet creating an injury such as a blister or aching pain for you. **Thumbs are often used to balance the ball just prior to release.**

Thumbs should be comfortably snug, but not tight. **If you truly want to add revs to your ball**, you should practice slightly balancing the ball on the back of your thumb throughout your swing and at release for those who spin the ball. Just prior to release the weight of the ball transfers to the finger joints or finger pads, to turn the ball, lift the ball and to rotate and deliver the spin onto the lanes.

Remember to open your hand and lift your thumb up to the ceiling. This is why some bowlers have slide tape on the back of their thumbs. They do not grab the ball, or squeeze. They may make the thumb stiff and slide the ball off it just by quickly unhinging the thumb knuckle during release.

Good bowlers learn the art of ejecting the thumb and getting it out very quickly for increased revs and better carry. **"Simple exercise"** – Bowlers should be able to slowly swing the bowling ball front to back with just the thumb in the ball without it falling to the floor.

No fingers are inserted to make this simple check. Just a slight flex of the thumb should be all that is required to keep the ball on the thumb during the backswing, especially for **end-over-end bowlers.**

End-over-End bowlers (advanced) will use a little bit of forward pitch in their thumbs to allow the ball to stay on the thumb securely through the backswing. Those who cup the ball with their thumbs pointing downward to the floor will often have more forward pitch in their thumbs to hang on to the ball without it falling off also.

Thumbhole too tight today - When you are out on the lanes and your ball comes off your hand and goes into the right gutter, the culprit could be that the thumbhole is too tight. This coupled with a very oily head condition will send the ball off your hand **later** than normal causing you to pull the shot out to the right. **Swelling of the thumb causes this also.**

If your ball seems to keep heading out to the right gutter at release then check your thumbhole and see if things are just a little bit too snug, you may want to take some tape out or open the thumbhole up just a little. If your ball continues to head out to the right gutter because your are using a **spinning release**, but the ball **feels** okay, try change immediately to the end-over-end release, this will definitely get your out of the gutter **and back into play.**

Thumbhole too big today - For whatever reason, you keep going Brooklyn or to the left of the headpin for a right handed bowler. The ball feels somewhat okay however, it could be that you are loosing the ball off your hand just a bit **too early.** If you have reverse pitch in on your thumb or left pitch, it could be the reason. However if you like the way the ball **feels** but think it may be falling off of your hand today, then add a piece of tape to the thumb hole on the right side of the hole, for right handers. Adding a piece of tape here will not change your span, and will bring the shot back to the right. **Remember, ball falls off to the right=tight thumb! Ball falls off to the Left = Loose thumb!**

Placing tape on the forward side of the thumbhole - When you place tape on the forward side of the thumbhole (the side away from you, but closer to the fingers) it will most likely start to affect the span between your fingers and thumb directly. **For instance, you place two pieces of tape in-line with your ring finger you will definitely feel the connection between your thumb and ring finger get tighter,** this may equal more turn or spin on your shot. Move the two pieces of tape to the left around towards the middle finger and "bam!" all of a sudden you may have more "lift" and backend reaction.

Of course, it depends on the bowler in any circumstances what will really happen when you move the tape, but this is a general example of what may happen to most bowlers. **(You may have to remind yourself throughout my book that I make good points to be considered, however they are based on <u>what release is the bowler using to deliver the ball.</u>)**

Placing tape on the reverse side or backside of the thumbhole - Ideally, you do not really want to change the span or feel of the ball at all. You want that ball to feel the way it does every time you are rolling the ball great and scoring great. For those times you just need to snug things up a little without affecting the shot to the left or to the right, **placing black tape to the back of the thumbhole is best. (If you have room place a piece of black tape on top of a piece of white tape in the thumbhole).**

Again, this does not change the span and allows for a continued clean release because of the slickness of the black tape. There is always a new invention in bowling to assist the bowler – Thank God! **There is now a soft mess colored roll of adhesive (carpet like) tap you can put on the back of your thumb now!** It is very soft to the touch and allows a quick release of the thumb. Try it out. See if it helps you when the thumbhole feels a little loose.

The damage thumb nerve at the base of your thumb:

At the base of your thumb just above the greater crease is an area (that after a short time of rubbing it **with a span that is too long for you**, or too wide) it will give way to great pain and discomfort. **Remember the body will only take so much.**

To remedy this most bowlers have three options. The **first** option is to **use bevel** to relieve pressure on the edge of the thumbhole. **Pivoting at the thumb joint and scrapping the nerve is what is causing the injury. Second,** you can simply put in a larger thumb "slug" that will allow you to bevel the edge just for you. (The best option) The larger sizes can be 1 1/4 and 1 3/8th of an inch slugs - **not necessarily vinyl inserts**.

This image is before the cut down of the thumb slug.

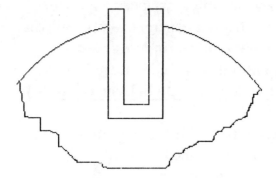

The image below is after the cut down of the thumb slug. The top edges **still** can be **elevated** extending the span at the base of the thumb and injuring the bowler.

Beveling, trims down, and smoves out the sharp edges. The pro shop staff can use a three sided **bevel knife** to lower the elevation.

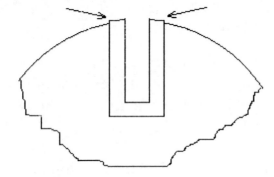

The below image shows a good cut down and minor beveling to smooth out the inside edges of the thumbhole.

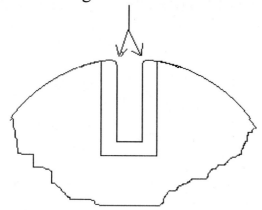

The image on the next page shows even better bevel with the attempt to provide a smoother exit for the thumb for those who squeeze the ball to deliver it to the pins. Unfortunately, this is the spot the ball has a tendency to pivot on, and it takes its toll on the nerve at the base of the thumb. *Do not squeeze the ball, just **set your hand.***

This injury may cause you to loose the ball in your swing. Noted tingling and sharp painful releases will often cause most bowlers to come out of the ball in almost a full roller style of release often **just to get the thumb out of the ball**. This release will sometimes **put the thumb below the fingers at release** just to get the thumb out the ball cleanly. The fingers will pull the ball backwards sometimes causing the oil track lines to travel across the finger hold or in the middle of the span.

If you bevel the ball and go throw a couple of shots and it **feels** better, do not stop there. Bevel a little more until there is no pressure there.

Once you are pain free, your fit should be monitored for a few weeks. Your targeting, release and timing will improve substantially. Most importantly, your pain should go away also.

(Best beveling to free pressure on thumb nerve.)

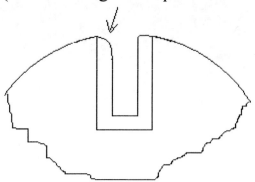

Lastly**, learn to get away from squeezing the ball by balancing the ball on the back of your thumb until you are ready to transfer the ball to the hand and fingertips for more revs than you ever thought you could ever do. Remember the fingertips are generally stiff and curled to the back walls of the finger holes inside the ball.**

Sore Thumbs - Most bowlers who have sore thumbs complain of an ache that is occurring. I have observed that while most of the cranker type bowlers or tweeners do have great hand in the ball for unleashing power to the pins, it can take a toll on the thumb. Often, the ball is being released repeatedly from a very low position. In addition, the ball is quite "tight" on the thumb. Likewise, the fingers are tight also. Raising the ball to a higher position at the start will alleviate a tremendous amount of discomfort and allow you to throw with about the same amount of revs.

Less revs from a high rev bowler is not a bad thing, especially when pain is avoided, and you still get as much snap at the backend as before. Remember to balance the ball on the back of the thumb more as you prepare to deliver the ball, and then let your fingers rip the rack!

"CAUTION"
I recommend these notes as only additional information to try <u>in practice</u> <u>to increase your skill level</u> and for you to "see" if it changes <u>your ball</u> reaction.

Trunk of the body- Leaning forward and leaning back. Simply stated, being a True bowler, you will often make whatever adjustments are necessary to get the ball to the pins consistently. If you find you are not getting to the pins from your normal up right position, "lean forward." Do not bend to the side.

The point here is to speed up the delivery. If you need to slow yourself down you can always **<u>lean back for great balance at the start.</u>** However, **you must know your body position to effectively repeat shots.**

Knees- As a coach, I'm not a real fan of fully erect bowlers when it comes to bent knees, especially for tall bowlers. Adjusting to keep the ball from bouncing on the lanes is a slight concern. Accuracy to the pins because of the bounce is the major concern. If you are accurate delivering the ball without it bouncing, there is no adjustment to be made. Otherwise, find a good starting balance, exercise consistent proper separation of your feet at the finish, have a good supportive hand position, following through when releasing the ball at a lower levels this will allow you to "roll" over your targets more consistently.

Knees and balance at the line. Often you may loose your balance at the line after delivering the ball. Please note that your slide knee should be bent, and that your head does not normally pass the slide knee. **To have good balance at the line, the trail leg knee should close right behind the slide leg knee** and not be overly exaggerated towards the non-ball side.

Again, bringing the trail leg knee **into the back of the slide leg knee will center you** and prevent excessive knee twisting at the foul line. This will help facilitate putting the trail leg toe either straight down behind you, or setting it down and pointing the toe to the non ball side as you finish your slide and delivery. **<u>Balance at the line is the point.</u> If you do not fall off your shot then there is no issue regardless of how you look at the line. Does not matter if your leg is down, or up in the air the majority of the time. "You just need to be balanced at the line." Balance** will allow you to watch the ball travel down the lane every time, **so you can read the ball's reaction!**

Feet - (Your feet and arm swing control the speed of the ball).
Adjustments with the feet vary from person to person, system to system. When instructing bowlers I have put "speed" in a format you can hopefully identify with. Feet position and balance with your first steps are preferred to be **consistently short** and **with good tempo** when possible. How you get to the foul line does not have to be textbook, but less is better. Overdoing it for **"show"** purpose defeats any adjustment we could ever address. Though it may look fancy, **fancy rarely is repeatable** for consistent and increased scores.

Scenario - Foot speed and arm swing control the speed of the ball across the foul line. For example: Walking slow and taking 3 seconds to release the ball is slow speed. However, walking slow and taking only 2 seconds to release that same length of swing means the ball goes faster out onto the lane. Walking faster and swinging slow is often counter productive. Basically, you get to the line and stop to wait for the ball to come down in the swing. Always time your actions so you do not to have to wait too long on the ball to swing through. Your tempo is the key to good speed.

Helpful hints to Fast and Slow Foot Speed: When speed is either increased or decreased, both actions "must" be followed through or the action will server to cancel out each other. **For example:** you walk faster to the release point however when you get there, it takes you three times as long to deliver the ball on to the lanes. The point here is: You cannot get to the release point and then not release the ball, so timing is everything. So practice, practice, practice! When slowing the shot down, you cannot walk slow to the line and then suddenly take a "long quick" power step to deliver the ball!

Feet Odd Steps Verses Even Steps - 5 step verses 4 step delivery - When executing the 4 step approach, **you have to worry about the ball immediately during your approach** which takes away from targeting somewhat. With the 5-step approach, you will note that **the target is your primary concern and you can focus more on reading your ball reaction and break point.** You would do well to **learn both** and keep both points in perspective. **Always aspire to keep it simple!**

Feet adjustments steps to go "slow": If you want to **slow** your ball down to read the reaction take **shorter steps** and **increase the number of steps** to the release point. To slow the ball travel down the lane you can **also** take long/slow deliberate steps as awkward as it may be. Here again, **"thinking"** slow or fast speed is the key. The **number of steps becomes irrelevant** in the big picture of things. **The point is as long as you arrive at the foul line slower or faster than you did before.**

This is just an opportunity for you as a bowler to experiment with a one of the adjustment keys to success by altering the number of your steps.
Special Note: Practice the 5 step _and_ the 4 step approach! You will be surprised to find that when you are over shooting your break point at the back of the lane, **REDUCING** the number of steps you take, will often bring you back into the pocket even though you are still starting from the same spot on the approach. **This is the "FIRST" adjustment you can make to figure out brake point to the pocket in terms of length of the shot.**

This adjustment when utilized becomes a lifesaver on many conditions and works well as conditions begin to change. **As the carry down increases, you can shorten your number of steps. Conversely, as the lanes dry out you can increase the number of steps for more length on the ball.**

MENTAL GAME!!! – Whenever you are practicing with others and someone else on various lanes near you throws good deliveries (spinning, end-over-end, etc.) with good reaction, take note of how many steps they may be taking to get to the pocket. Even if you are just standing around watching a tournament or league play, take note of how many steps to the pocket bowlers are taking when they deliver a good shot with their delivery. <u>Bowling is a speed sensitive sport.</u>

CHECKING THE HEADS FOR OIL - VISUAL OBSERVATION
<u>Always notice the head oil by just walking up and checking the approach foul line area where you can look down and see oil on the heads from 10 to 10 or somewhere around there. Especially, if you like to play the outside edges of the lanes near the channel. Check to see where the oil begins 2 inches to 6 inches from the foul line.</u> **Also, check to see if the head oil is dry, spotty, glossy, wet or very shiny looking like wet water.**

Coaches will show you these area differences during lessons by walking you down the side of the lanes to show you the oil patterns and the pin deck. USBC Certified Instructors will often have no problem obtaining permission from the bowling center manager to provide this very necessary service.

Standing in the right spot on the approach: Often standing in the right spot is a matter of **are you willing to move to score higher if needed?** For most bowlers **we do not want to move!** We dig in like ticks and try to make where we are standing on the approach our home. This is fine if you have all the adjustment tools in your mental bag of tricks. (See information regarding Truebowler's **"Bowling Coach in a bag,** help card."
www.TrueBowlerAdjustments.com)
In order for you not to move from your target line, you would have to have a diverse arsenal of cores and covers for varying lane conditions.

For you not to move, you need to be aware of **the release you are using.** In addition, you need to be aware of **your ball height** or position in your approach stance. You have to **know where you are standing** on each approach because the lanes may be different by a few feet of reaction.

If your ball is going Brooklyn, you may want to insure you point your slide foot heel and toe, the direction you want to go when you begin moving to the foul line! Especially, when you deliver the ball at the foul line. Keep your slide foot heel and toe pointed in the direction you want to deliver the ball. This is extremely important.

This keeps your foot from sliding in one direction when your arm is swinging in the opposite direction. Lastly, concerning your feet, **you may have to move up or move back** to change the reaction of the ball.
Feet movement stepping back - "Getting the ball further down the lane": Often times you will hear the comment "Lay the ball down in the heads. It will go longer down the lane" The Heads of the lanes or the "skid" part of the lane **"should be"** oily. Stepping back 6" or 1 foot may allow you to get into more oil, allowing your ball to carry further down the lane, without changing your target in front of you, as long as your speed is up.

Feet movement - Stepping up on the approach "Getting the ball to react sooner on the lane": Step up 6" to 1 foot, will help you to get out of heavy oil. How far up depends on you, there is no set area for delivering the ball. If you end up using a three-step approach 4 feet from the foul line, just be consistent. **Especially,** when it gets you out of the oil with good reaction. Again, with moving up on the approach, often times you do not have to change your target. Moving up, will kick out the 5-pin, or 5 / 7 pin leaves sometimes when there is **reverse buff** on the lanes. Reverse buff will often provide a **hold spot** for the ball, which will **increase the distance the ball travels at the backend.** Using a stable drilling or a ball pinned some where above your fingers. Often an **end-over-end release** will help to defeat this condition. A spinning release can be used when the 10 pin begins **to fall last, or remain standing.** Usually you will suspect the heads to be dry at that point also. You can set the ball down early in the heads with the spinning release and get a "longer roll" into the pins using the same line.

Feet movement side-to-side "Moving side to side to get reaction on the ball": There are several adjustments "side to side" to get the ball to react sooner, or later down the lanes.

First, we must discuss the old school thoughts on adjustments concerning blocked shots **(oil from 10 to 10 across).** When seeking a shot solution for your lane, go to where you like to stand and deliver your ball as best as you can the first time and check for a reaction.

Watch whether your ball goes to the left really early (goes too short), or whether it goes to the right, missing the headpin (too long). If either of these happens, you will have to "adjust."

I am sure you have seen others throw countless strikes in practice and loose the "edge" during the game. Did those individuals really check to see how fast they were walking to the line to deliver the ball? Probably not. In that light, now they want to adjust to the left or the right to compensate for the ball going too long or the ball coming up too short.

Truebowler recommends adjustments for both. Keep in mind; do not to use up your spot where you land the ball on the lane in practice! The adage **"don't use up all your strikes in practice"** before league holds **very true!** You will deplete the oil in your sweet spot if you keep throwing the ball there over and over requiring you to have to move a lot sooner than you anticipated.

First, very few people throw the ball up the 10 board anymore. Choose a couple of boards to the left or right side of the 10 board and deliver your shots there first. **Others use the 10 board so often and it becomes very worn during play.** All too frequently, the 10 board will dry out sooner and make the ball hook earlier requiring you to change your line. Thus, now you have to move left or right of the 10 board.

Never discount using the 10 board either. Play the 10 board only if you have enough oil without lots of effort on your part, to get the ball to the head pin. Use the 10 board when you need to hook the ball more into the pocket after half a game or so if others have been playing it. **The pros will often use the 10 board in the first part of practice to try to line up a shot.** You should do the same along with trying at least two places to stand near by the 10 board to deliver your shot. Also, try your A-Game release and your B-Game release there in practice.

Side to side movement - To get the ball to go longer: When the ball is consistently diving through the middle of the rack either Brooklyn or taking out the head pin leaving splits and such, it is coming in too high. Most often factors are such that you must find enough oil to get to the pocket.

For the house shot oiled from 10 to 10: Move your feet 2 boards left and keep your same target. If that does not work, then you will want to **step up from your new starting position about 3 to 6 inches** and use **the same target**. Do not make big moves, until you are more experienced. Moving left and up with the same target will get the ball out to the right side of the headpin normally. You can make this move up to three times I have noticed (if you have room on the approach) before you get into a little trouble with the ball "squirting" into the carry down. So if you see a light hit that carries, your next move left may not be so fruitful. Still it takes courage to bowl well. **Feet side to side:** Use a system and practice it, moving (1 by 1), (2 by 1), (2 to 2), (3 to 3) etc; side to side moves with your feet. The first number moves your feet, and the second number moves your target on the lane. It gets more complicated than back to front moves because you begin to cross boards and change your entry angle. **Not a bad thing,** however, you will experience that **you don't have as much pocket carry the further left you move** (right handed) and the ball may tend to roll out on you more leaving more 10 pins or 5/10's (oily lanes) **depending on the release you are using**. It is best to use a system that works for you.

Moving your feet 1 board, 2 boards, or 3 boards is acceptable. Likewise, moving your targets on the lanes 1 board, 2 boards, or 3 boards is acceptable. However, **it is not recommend to make big moves** such as 5 to 7 boards unless you are **experienced. You have an established arsenal,** consistent **releases,** and **a solid game plan** for doing so.

Often a 3 board move on the approach is equal to a 2 board change at the pins.

If in **heavy oil,** with some hook, **moving parallel** left of your previous lay down and target is fine (example 2 boards to the left on the approach, by 2 boards down lane, to the left of your original target).

If you are in a **medium to dry oil** predicaments, you know because your ball hooks, or it hooks a lot! When you move side to side with your feet, you often are changing the entry angle for a better carry or strike ball. The system of moving your feet 2 boards and moving your target on the lane 1 board is one system of adjustment.

The point here is, every bowler needs to **find a system** of adjustment, no matter if the combinations are 1 to 0, 2 to 0, 2 to 1, or 2 to 2, etc. **Find the angle to the pocket that works for you.** As you advance, you will note three distinct **patterns** of play. You will move up to play an area. Another lane condition will require you to move back.

All conditions will require you to moving left until your ball squirts through the rack; you run out of room moving to the left; you realize the middle is too dry to play there; or, lastly you will have to move right.

As you move right, your hand position may have to change. In addition, your lay down and ball surface may have to change, as well as your speed. Having **a game plan** is extremely important.

Very Important! <u>Never be too far away from the pocket!</u> <u>Most bowlers do not know how to get closer to the head pin. To get closer to the head pin you can move left one board (and if you have room) you can move up 3 to 6 inches using the same target. If you are far up on the approach and need to get closer to the pocket you can step straight back and move your target left 1 to 2 boards, this will cause you to throw straighter down lane instead of swinging the ball out to the channel. Flatten out your wrist as you throw more direct to the pins.</u>

If you are going Brooklyn! The combination of moving left 1 board or 2 boards and moving up 3 to 6 inches, <u>using a single target will give you more angles to get further to the right if you are going Brooklyn.</u>   This coupled with opening your shoulder up, concentrating more pressure on your ring finger, using a little ball tilt, and finishing your swing at 1 o'clock (right handed) may push the ball further to the correct side of the headpin.

Feet and the separation of the feet: Whatever your balance is when you are standing on the approach, well - that is just how you start your delivery. That is the balance that is working for you, however, when you are standing on the approach and you just can't seem to get going because **your feet** are toe to toe, side by side, parallel and even, and you just seem to rock back and forth, separate your feet and bend your knees a bit.

Just simply drop your right foot (right handed) back 2 to 3 inches and rebalance at the start point. This will allow you to relax and like a runner, you will find the more separation you employ, the faster you will get to the foul line as an adjustment.

Feet Conclusion – Feet Separation at the Foul line.

<u>**Your feet help you stay on-line to your target**</u>
    A short step, spacing, or short separation of your feet at the foul line may often cause you to release early and go Brooklyn. This is most evident when someone "sticks" on the approach. This will often anger many bowlers who rely on separation of their feet for **a proper release**. Often these bowlers have mastered repeating their shots to get good reaction out of the ball, regardless of their averages. If a bowler experiences a shorter than normal slide step, it will slow your ball. This may cause an early reaction down lane, which will often come up short of your intended targets.

Proper feet separation at the foul line, will often help you to hit your targets more precisely. An **over extended separation** of the feet at the line may cause the ball **to skid excessively**, it often pushes more outside of your targets and you'll overthrow the breakpoint quite often. Finding your proper foot separation at delivery is **a key to repeating your shot!**

Established to Advanced Bowler Adjustments 150 – 170 average

THE BALL

SPEED AND BALL SELECTION

People speed, equals ball selection - Most individuals do pretty much the same things every time they throw the ball down the lanes. Basically, bowlers move very fast, moderately fast, or slow with our deliveries.

Our people speed tells us that if we go slow, we will often need a bowling ball that **does not** have a heavy core or large core, because the ball may hook and roll out too soon. Likewise, if our delivery is very fast and we spin the ball to rip the cover off, we cannot very well use something that is hard and slick like plastic with no core inside, because it will never hook in time and will skid well past the break point or dry area on the lane.

Based on how fast you deliver your ball you should seek a ball that compliments your speed to the foul line and **hopefully, it will read the lanes well enough to allow you increased distance down the lane before hooking.** So if you are very slow **go with a ball that has a small core or puck inside** with a reactive cover or plastic ball.

If you are a **cranker** (someone who really spins the ball), you may need **something that has a larger core** and softer cover that will read the lanes sooner because of how **fast** you deliver and spin the ball **to the backend.**

Is the ball light enough for you to use? Are you sacrificing accuracy? In selecting a bowling ball always remember one thing - a 15-pound ball is a 15-pound ball, regardless if the core is small or large. A ball that is too heavy eventually will hurt you and your game.

"When" your ball hooks is a matter of your people speed, how large or heavy the core is, lane conditions, surface preparation, and the ball layout.

Another factor, where you project the ball out onto the lanes, is known as **your lay down spot.** Your laydown spot is approximately, where the ball crosses the foul line on its way to your first target.

You can feel much more comfortable throwing **a ball light enough for you.** This lighter, smaller core ball, 13 or 14 lb ball will retain a lot of energy for the backend. You will not tire out, as soon. **You will last a lot longer than having a bowling ball that is too heavy, hooks, then rolls out way too soon on the lane.**

Bowling Ball Dynamics

The ball: To understand bowling balls, you have to understand people. People are like the bowling balls they use. The bowling balls today come in all sorts. Light to heavy, colorful to plain, hard to soft, and with today's bowling balls you can even get balls that are unscented and scented that smell like grapes, berries, or even chocolate!

Let's talk about light to heavy bowling balls. **Nothing, and I do mean nothing, hampers a bowler's ability to adjust on the lane as much as trying to throw a bowling ball that is too heavy!**

I would love for the language used in addressing the customer's needs, to be changed to: **"Is this light enough for you to bowl with?"** rather than: "Is this heavy enough for you?" Find a ball that is light enough for you to roll down the lanes. Enough said hear because this could get really long winded...

Next, colorful to plain. Find a ball you like looking at, seriously. Most pro shops will carry very nice bowling balls. Bowling balls can be drilled to match your **speed** and **your release** (that is, if the pro shop staff asks you how you deliver or release the ball). I hope that you will purchase a ball that **you can see rolling or spinning/turning** as it is going down the lane (multicolored). **Solid dark colored balls** require and eagle's eye to watch for good ball reactions. **It is easier to see the ball tracks on dark colored bowling balls.** If nothing else, you can always add lighter colored finger and thumb inserts to watch ball travel.

If they have a limited supply, pro shops often carry catalogs and will order what you need/want. A good pro shop will be able to drill the bowling ball to suit the type of ball reaction you need. On-line purchases are cheaper however; it will cost you to take the bowling ball in, to get it drilled.

When it comes to hard or soft, this is the point you scratch your head and go, huh? Hard or soft refers to the **outside of the ball.** If the cover or shell of the ball is soft, it is more likely to have a heavy and large core to it. This heavy and larger core is designed to make the ball "hook" early. The softer shell or cover is designed to provide more friction as well as soaking up oil on the lanes. This allows the ball to grab the lanes sooner and hold the line.

Balls "covers and cores": A ball that "hooks" early is not a good thing for a "slow" bowler that has a good ball reaction. Bowlers, who are very slow, are buying the high-end balls wanting them to **"hook a lot,"** unfortunately - they are getting exactly what they are asking for sometimes. Especially if they do not have any idea how **they are releasing the ball.**

These balls do hook a lot, however they hook too early and can make you a career 135 to 150 bowler, if not drilled properly for your delivery.

What you see after you deliver these high-end smashing machines is a bowling ball that has hooked and rolled out after only 10 to 15 feet of travel and **now it is on a straight line to the pins where ever it hits.** It **looks like it is hooking to the pins** but, it is just rolling towards them pretty much on a straight line.

It has hooked very early, the revs have maxed out, and the ball has rolled out. Hopefully, it will arrive at the pocket and carry because it hit the right spot on the head pin, which will be mostly toward the center and not to the outside of the head pin.

If you think about it, this is not a problem either especially as you get better at reading your delivery. There is always something that will work for someone in bowling. If it works for you, fine.
Large core balls can make a great control balls for a slow bowler who consistently delivers to that one target on the lanes, or to their targets on the lane **with a good release. (i.e. End-over-end, spinning, full roller, or back up ball).** *This great when you know a particular bowling house oils the length of the oil conditioner pretty much the same, week to week.*

In bowling, a Truebowler tries **EVERYTHING!** Soft cover, heavy or larger cores are often the choice of highly athletic bowlers who turn the ball very well. Many manufactures today control the weight of the ball by varying the composite material used in the cover of the ball as well.

Highly athletic bowlers often have virtually no problem getting the ball down the lane to the pins every time. Ball travel is not a problem, whether they have a lot of oil, or just a little. **(See illustration #1)**

Large Core - 3 piece bowling ball - 1= Large core, 2 = inner material covering the core, and 3 = the outer bowling ball shell.

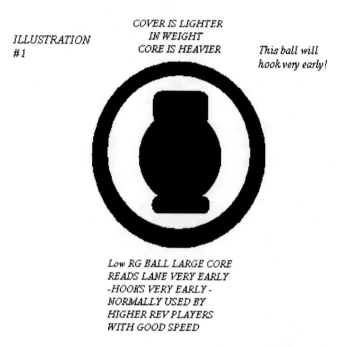

ILLUSTRATION #1

COVER IS LIGHTER IN WEIGHT CORE IS HEAVIER

This ball will hook very early!

Low RG BALL LARGE CORE READS LANE VERY EARLY -HOOKS VERY EARLY - NORMALLY USED BY HIGHER REV PLAYERS WITH GOOD SPEED

TrueBowlerAdjustments.com

Now if the cover of the ball is a medium cover that means its cover can be harder by its make up properties than the previous soft cover ball. In addition, the weight of the **cover can be heavier** whereas the **core is a touch lighter** in weight, or size as far as dynamics are concerned.

The main thing to remember is medium balls are **even** in **core and cover** weight basically, may have a harder outer shell which will not grab the lane and hook as early as the heavy core soft shell ball previously talked about. Also, **with today's technology outer shell hardness is often very small in differences, making most bowling balls of the same general hardness.** The real difference lies in the porosity of the cover. In other words, how big the tiny holes or craters are on the surface. What you will find **very important,** is knowing **what ball layout to use at different times** to be most helpful.

For Medium Bowling Balls, (See illustration #2)

The cover and core of a medium ball are often of equal weight. The ore of a medium ball is small than the previous ball and will go further before hooking.

Illustration #2

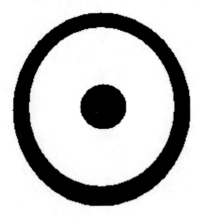

MEDIUM BALLS WILL OFTEN READ THE LANE ABOUT HALF WAY DOWN BEFORE HOOKING.

TrueBowlerAdjustments.com

High RG Bowling Balls go longer down the lane, (See illustration #3) Today's bowling balls may even incorporate a core that is more horizontal to increase the rev rate of their product. It take more to spin a core that stands up and down in a bowling ball verses spinning the core of a ball when it is more horizontally configured.

ILLUSTRATION #3   *May have no center core or the core may be horizontal in presentation. The cover is reactive to hook on the backend. - Ball goes long.*

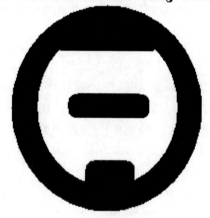

HIGH RG BALL
OFTEN WITH
HARDER COVER
TO GO FARTHER
DOWN THE LANE
PRIOR TO HOOKING

TrueBowlerAdjustments.com

This lighter core weight will "skid" further, "hook" later, and "roll" into the pins with lots of stored energy. **High RG ball's center cores are often more horizontal in profile also.**

Dry Ball -Let's imagine you walk out to the approach, look out onto the lanes and you see nothing but haziness on the lanes and in the heads. There is no glossy or shininess to the lanes whatsoever. Basically, it is dry as the Sahara desert. Now you really need a ball that is cover hard and will not hook much at all. It needs to have very little in the center core so it doesn't "hook" until it gets to the backend.**(See illustration #3)** It basically needs to "skid" forever until it really hit's the very dry backend. Still this ball can have a reactive cover that has some "hook" potential. Slow bowlers that approach the line smoothly at a slower pace need High RG bowling balls **that will not burn up on the front end** usually. Employing a flip drilling will allow the ball **to finish hooking and roll into the pins at the backend.**

Using what it takes to raise your scores is the goal of a Truebowler. (TIP) - When bowling dry lanes, release bowling ball from a higher position into the lane. Lower releases finish well. However, may hook too early at times!

Plastic Balls: When it comes to covers and cores, there is the ultimate straight ball that is made of polyester and has no weight block for its core per se.` This ball will generally move one to two boards if any at all when rolled 60 feet down the lane. Overall, as you bowl and gain more experience, you will find your speed, and your ball speed. You will find in the numbers how hard your shell of the ball needs to be, and how light or heavy the core needs to be. This combination of numbers called "RG". These Radius of Gyration factors and differentials will consistently get you to the pins. You may also find that only two types of bowling balls work for you. You may find Particle Pearl balls to be your best friend or you may love the control that reactive resin provides you. You may find that the different conditions you bowl on warrants that you have 4 balls in your arsenal with different backend reaction layouts or as many as 6 bowling balls, **especially if you have only one type of release. However, for picking up spares, a plastic ball is King!**

Balls Covers and cores: No matter how many bowling balls you own, they have to "clear the heads and react on the backend!"

4 types of balls and what they do.
Polyester - straight, no hook, all skid
Urethane - long skid, continuous long hook, and roll
Reactive Resin - will skid; will hook at a point on the lane and roll out.
Particle Pearlized Reactive - will skid, clear dry heads, will hook/snap in midlane harder than reactive resin, before rolling out.

Final words about having **too heavy a ball in your hands:**
ABSOLUTELY NOTHING, is better than having a ball in your hands that
is light enough for you to throw. A ball light enough you so that you can put
lots of revolutions on it, be able to change hand release positions with it,
and change ball positions (height - raising or lowing the ball in your stance)
without incurring discomfort. Overall, one of the most important factors that
is over looked is bowling is the **laydown. Your laydown is your ability to
land the ball in a certain spot time and time again, as the ball crosses
the foul line.** Sometimes this spot is close to you and **sometimes you will
have to project the ball farther out** onto the lanes. However, where you
cross the foul line with your ball is your laydown area. **The assumption** is
that you will land the ball in the same spot during all three games
horizontally across the lanes and **this is not the case in bowling,** especially
after the lanes begin to transition. Having **a light enough ball** that you can
manipulate at the foul line **is priceless. This is a key to repeating shots.**

Ball Purchases – I have seen countless good bowlers matched up with good
balls that produced **very bad games.** Again, you are saying "What the
...?" It is true, you can have a good bowler and a great ball but they are a
terrible match!

 Being a consistent bowler with a ball that rolls over your target but
hooks and rolls out "before" midlane is terrible. There are no revs to "mix"
pins on the backend, and you only have accuracy to the headpin as a saving
grace "depending" on the lane conditions.
 Opposite of that is having a ball that reads the lane too late. This will
just frustrate you, causing bucket after bucket leaves on the lane.
 Simply put, if you walk really fast to the foul line to deliver the ball and
you turn the heck out of the ball or try to rip the cover off it as they say,
others will label you a **cranker.** You have Truebowler's blessings to go out
and buy that $250 bowling ball! You will need that soft or pearlized cover to
clear the dry heads, dig into the oil at the midlane, and bring your shot
back crushing the pins as only you can do it !!!

 If you just so happen to be fortunate enough to have **good foot speed**
and great hand coming out of the ball like we see most of the pros on TV
you are probably a **"tweener"** or power stroker. Someone in between a
cranker and a stroker. First advice to all tweeners .... **FIND A COACH
and work with him or her to learn adjustments** unless True Bowler
Adjustments works just fine for you!

Tweeners can use any bowling ball!!! Since generally you will not have any trouble getting to the pocket you can concern yourself with ball reaction and whatever your pocketbook can afford. **Remember, find a coach !!!**

Now on to the strokers. **Strokers** are a breed of their own. I like to think of strokers as those folks who truly want and have the desire to throw **"one ball"** and go back and sit down.

Strokers take just enough time to fine where to stand, position their hand in the ball, look at their target - Oh, I forgot, they check to see that no one is running up on the lane beside them and also three lanes over – etc.,etc, ... okay, back to buying a ball.

Strokers are normally slower in speed in the bowling track and field world. A stroker will generally purchase a ball costing $80 to $150 or lower priced. **If you are slow to the foul line, you need a ball that does NOT have a LARGE core to it more than likely.**

You will want a ball with a smaller core that will save its energy and save its revolutions to be used at the backend.

Purchasing a ball that has **a harder shell** or one that is **"cover heavy"** is a good investment for a stroker, also. Experience is always the true test of who can use any ball they possess. **Just remember strokers are generally slow getting to the foul line.** I have found that there is nothing tricky to the specs that manufacturers list concerning bowling balls.

When purchasing a ball, it will list the "RG" values for the cover and the core. Strokers need a cover RG that is high (2.60 to 2.70) if they are listed as such. The core value may be on a color scale that may go from cover heavy to core heavy. If not, you would be seeking a core value near below .40 to .35 as and average if not even lower.

CAUTION - These numbers or values are to be used only as just a guide - although this is just a general observation, your bowling experience should be highly enjoyable allowing you to get to the headpin without effort every time, as long as you have good timing !!!!.

Remember: These values allow your ball to store energy and skid further than other bowling balls that are virtually the same weight considering the harder and polished cover, and lesser influence of the core to make the ball hook earlier.

Ball Layouts – It is extremely important to "**know**" how the ball layout affects your shot. Keeping things simple, the pin or colored dot on the ball, always tries to move from its drilled position to a position either standing up or laying down as it travels down the lane.

You may see this pin on the left side of the ball spinning from a big to a smaller circle on the side of the ball as it travels down the lane. Then as the ball finishes hooking it will disappear, because now the ball is rolling straight away from you and the pin is on the side of the ball. Once **the pin** gets there it has lain down on the lanes like a broomstick rolling away from you and parallel to the lanes. Unfortunately, this ball can be **deflected.**

Some Truebowlers deliver the ball so that the pin is tumbling somewhat **end-over-end** at first going down the lane, **you will notice that the label colors on the ball and the finger holes will move from the right side of the ball during its travel, to the left side of the ball.** This is the pin's movement to "flare" and try to stand up, as it comes back to the pins due to the ball being tilted at release, prior to the pin lying back down.

Looking at the bowling ball (finger holes and the thumbholes facing you with the thumbhole at the bottom, and the two finger holes at the top side by side) most ball drillers will place the pin in the strongest position for you because you will say, **"I really want the ball to hook a lot for me!"**

What you will see is the color pin placed to the right of your ring finger. Below that you may see a small pin punch mark or a circle with a pin punch inside of it stacked below the pin about 1 to 2 inches below the colored pin.

This pin punch is called your **center of gravity** or **CG**. This CG pin punch does not have much of an effect on the ball unless you are a high tech bowler. (See illustration # 4)

This drill layout is **a continuous drilling**. It often places the pin in a position near the ring finger in which it travels down lane in a smooth curve.

This attempt to place the weight of the ball on the pulling side of the ball to bring it back into the pins as it travels down lane, thumb hole leading away from you down lane.

Most bowlers get into trouble with this drill when there is carry down in front of the three pin, and the headpin because the ball will not finish. It begins to leave the bucket or 2/4/5/8. It is because of the oil deposited there from the heads, causes the ball to come in light on the head pin. Lofting this layout will avoid the dry heads and hopefully allow the ball to finish on the backend. If not, the choice of a flip drilled ball would be more appropriate.

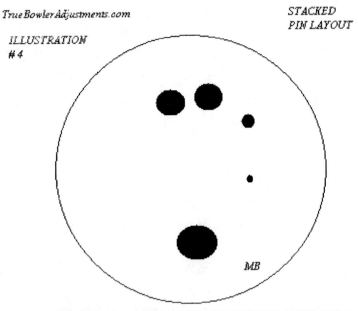

TrueBowlerAdjustments.com

STACKED PIN LAYOUT

ILLUSTRATION #4

MB

GENERALLY DISCRIBED AS THE STRONGEST LAYOUT FOR A BOWLER WHO HAS LOTS OF HAND REVOLUTIONS AND BALL SPEED. PROVIDES AWSOME RECOVERY FOR CRANKERS AND TWEENERS. STROKERS WHO MASTER BALL TILT CAN SCORE WELL PROVIDED THEY CAN DELAY THE HOOKING ACTION

However, if you use the stacked layout, remember to use the lowest grit preparation you can fine on heavy oil (180 to 300 grit). Then start going up until you can get good length out of the ball before it "hooks" back to the pocket. For house shots, between 350 to 2000 grit will allow you to read the balls reaction. The extremes sanding grits are design for use mostly in the driest house shot (4000), or the wettest conditions (180 to 300).

*** Special Note*** **Can you really tell how someone has prepared the surface of their bowling ball just by looking at it???**

No, you cannot! **You have to think outside of the box, so you can ADJUST.**

Bowling balls loose length of travel after 12 games when they are prepared for dry conditions because the surface becomes matted down and is no longer slick enough to support ball travel. Heat and friction melts things together and causes a tackiness that makes the ball hook more and more. ADJUSTMENT - <u>You must polish, (or if needed sand and polish) your bowling balls before league or tournament play!!!</u>

Likewise, bowling balls that have been prepared for oily lanes loose there hooking ability after 6 to 12 games because the surface becomes too smooth to grab the lanes. The excess oil makes the ball hydroplane or skid, so to speak. ADJUSTMENT - Again, - <u>You must sand or if needed polish your bowling balls before league or tournaments play !!!</u>

Polish can come in different grits, such as 800, 1000, 1500 to 3500 grits.

Figure out what ball surface prep you need, sanded or polished or a combinations of both, figure out your speed and delivery, and figure out what condition you normally play on and you will get the ball to the headpin the majority of the time. Use your A-Game release or B-Game release to get you to the headpin.

Mass Bias. Ohhhh yesss, this is the one key to ball reaction that will help you. Even though it may not be marked on the ball, the mass bias which is the heaviest part of the ball, is located from the colored pin through the pin punched CG (center of Gravity) out to 6 3/4 inches.

The Mass Bias and pin position will influence the reaction of the ball on the backend of the lane. Most notably, whether the ball smooth curves, or snaps hard on the backend, hooks on the backend, or arcs on the backend.

On most of the more expensive competitive bowling balls the Mass Bias will be identified by some type of logo. It can be offset from the CG to delay its hooking action also.

Focusing on the mass bias and the pin you can lay out your bowling ball to react strong with its layout and snap to the left at the midlane, or you can have your ball travel farther down the lane and hook as late as possible with the same strong snap back to the pins allowing the ball to rev up later down lane.

These are two separate actions from the ball. One action (placement of the pin) extends "ball travel." The other action is down lane "backend reaction" which depends on the placement of the pin and the Mass Bias.

Ball travel or length down the lane can be manipulated by moving the pin above the fingers. *In many ways the pin controls where your breakpoint is on the lane.*

Ball travel can also be increased by making the ball delay reaction by **additionally moving the pin to the left away from the ring finger towards the middle finger. This will let the ball get further down the lane** before turning or hooking towards the pins.

Conversely, if you bring the pin down below the fingers the ball will move much quicker to lie down on the lane. This action will cause the ball to hook or turn earlier and earlier the closer you place it to the pinky finger or outside the ring finger. Especially with **the end-over-end or forward roll release**.

As you learn more about bowling try to think about **what your ball does** on the lanes. **More specifically; does it go too long before hooking, does it hook too soon, does it not finish to the pocket, or does it just go straight with no reaction.** **What does your ball do**, and then, …what does it **NOT DO** for you? When a ball is pinned in a strong position (pinned down or under the ring finger) with a slow bowler, it will often hook too soon.** After contacting the lane, it will turn towards the pins and often will arrive at the pins "DOA" **dead on arrival** with no revolutions and no finishing force left to drive through the pins.

This will occur especially if the Mass bias is kicked out 45 degrees to the right, or anywhere right of the thumbhole for right-handed bowlers who deliver end-over-end releases.

It will deflect off the headpin and go around the 5 pin. This happens because the pin has lain completely down and deflects away to the right because it lacks the driving force of the pin moving forward into the pins coming out of its hooking stage and still digging into the lane. You may leave the 5-10 split, or the dreaded 10 pin by itself.

Ball Layouts -Finding a great ball layout that works for you may take a little effort but it is worth it. To make things easier Truebowler has listed 5 **mass bias** positions you may want to try on your bowling ball.

The **mass bias** in many ways help to control or "tweek" **when your ball revs up as it goes down the lane.** If it is to the far right (right handed) it will rev up **early** in the heads. If it is to the far left (right handed) it will rev up **later** down the lane.

Looking at your bowling ball with the fingers up and the thumbhole down ball facing you. The mass bias or heaviest part of the ball can be positioned on the left side of the ball from "0 degrees" which is straight across your palm with the pin on your "positive axis point" and your CG in the middle of your span or there about.

Then it can be moved counter clockwise down and under the thumb to the right side of the ball. As we move the mass bias we would like to move it in a number of degrees or in positions like the hands on a clock.

There is: ("0 degrees" or 9 o'clock position)   (See illustration #5),

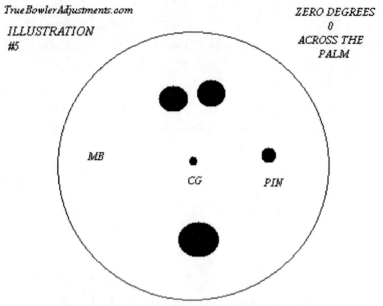

ZERO DEGREES
0
ACROSS THE
PALM

MB

CG   *PIN*

PLAYER CREATES BALL TILT THAT DIGS INTO THE
LANE OFTEN THE PIN IS SEEN THROUGHOUT BALL
TRAVEL UNTIL IT LAYS DOWN ON THE LANE HOOKING
INTO THE PIN DECK. PIN IS OFTEN PLACE ON "PAP"

Illustration #5 - The "0-degree" or 9 o'clock position places the pin on your Positive Axis Point - PAP. This PAP is where the pin always tries to migrate or come down to if you put the pin somewhere else on the ball. Since you are putting the pin here in the beginning, you'll have to learn to tilt and spin the ball as it leaves your hand. Otherwise, it will pretty much just roll down the

lane like a straight ball. (Drier lane conditions, up the middle out to 10 board.)

Although we speak of mass bias it is best to place the pin **close to** but not on the PAP.

("135 degrees" or 7 o'clock label drill position)**(See illustration #6),**

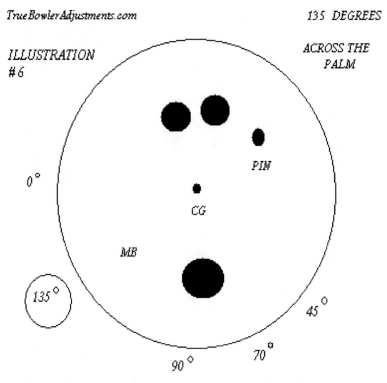

135 DEGREES

ILLUSTRATION
#6

ACROSS THE
PALM

PIN

0°

CG

MB

135°

45°

70°

90°

MOST VERSITAL LAYOUT - LABEL DRILL ACROSS THE PALM
-MASS BIAS LANDS ON THE BALL TRACK - ARCHING PATTERN
CAN BE OBSERVED WITH GOOD HAND ROTATION WHEN
STANDING LEFT OR DELIVERING OFF THE GUTTERS.

Illustration #6 - The 135 degrees or 7 o' clock position **is versatile.** The 135 degree or 7 o'clock "label" drill and the pro shops like to call it can be delivered from the extreme left of the approach with good hand, or from the extreme right side around the 1st arrow in light oil, up the gutter for outstanding carry through the pins. This drilling layout often delays the hooking action of the ball, giving it late revolutions, allowing length and skid down the lane ending in an arch like finish and "flip" through the pin deck, provided the pin is positioned close to your vertical axis line or VAL. ("90 degrees" or 6 o'clock drill position)**(See illustration #7),**

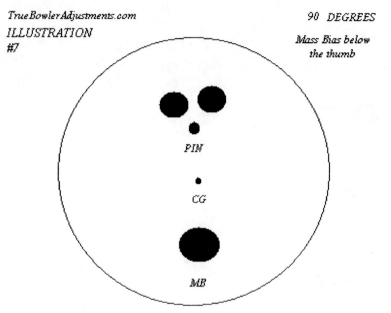

90 DEGREES

Mass Bias below
the thumb

GENERALLY CAN BE USED UP THE MIDDLE SHOTS
STAYING INSIDE 15 TO 10 BOARD WHEN THERE IS OUT OF
BOUNDS PASS THE 10 BOARD. PIN CAN BE PLACED HIGHER
FOR INCREASED LENGTH ON DRIER INSIDE AREAS

Illustration # 7 - The 90-degree or 6 o'clock drill layout is described as the inside shot layout. This layout can be used when you like to play, or have to play up the middle of the lane in long oil to get that snap and carry when anything outside of 15/10 boards leaves wash outs or won't come back to the pocket because of high oil or carry down. **Kicking the pin out 1" to 2"** from your ring finger will give you a FLIP drilling that will finish with a violent reaction. 90 degree is a more stable roll, spinning release or end-over-end released.

("70 degrees" or 5 o'clock position just to the right side of the thumbhole)

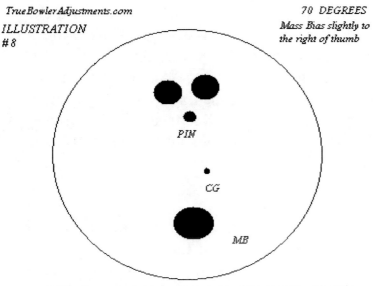

ILLUSTRATION
#8

70 DEGREES
*Mass Bias slightly to
the right of thumb*

PIN

CG

MB

GENERALLY CAN BE PLAYED STRAIGHT UP THE TRACK AREA
OR STRAIGHT UP 15 BOARD

The 45-degrees or 4 o'clock to 4:30 position **(See illustration #9).**

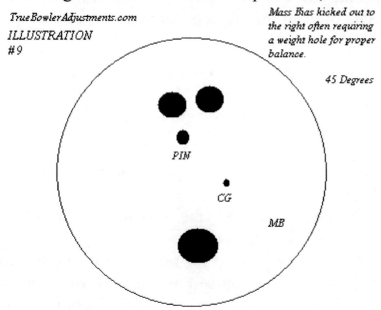

TrueBowlerAdjustments.com
ILLUSTRATION
#9

*Mass Bias kicked out to
the right often requiring
a weight hole for proper
balance.*

45 Degrees

PIN

CG

MB

GENERALLY CAN BE PLAYED STRAIGHT UP THE TRACK AREA
CLOSER TO THE 10/12 BOARD. THIS LAYOUT IS OFTEN THE
STRONGEST LAYOUT FOR STROKERS WITH GREAT
BACKEND REACTION

Illustration #9 - The 45 degree or 4 o'clock or 4:30 mass bias position often is used for track players who deliver the ball around 2nd arrow or around the 15th to the 10th board on the lane.

The 45-degree layout provides the strongest backend reaction for most strokers who deliver an end-over-end release. It also gives the earliest revs on the ball as it contacts the lane. It can be varied by moving the layout up, or to the left depending on the distance between the pin and the CG. The higher you place the pin above the fingers the longer the distance has to be between the pin and the CG. Keep the CG in the center of the grip as much as possible. Balls, 3 to 4 inch pin outs (distance from the pin to the CG) work best for placing the pin above the fingers to get distance down the lane on a ball.

Final Words on Layouts: Overall, the experts for the ball layouts are **the pro shop staffers. (As Richard Jenkins of Las Vegas, NV. would say, "pro shop personnel are the hardware guys!")** However, see for yourself what others are throwing on the lanes.

Find your coach!   (*According to Richard, - "Coaches are the Software* **Guys!")** Thanks Richard....

Coaches work on the people part of bowling, the physical training. Pay attention, and compensate coaches for helping you to be a success.

A wise person once said "to be successful at something, the simplest way to achieve this is to find someone else who does what you want to do, and ask them to show you how to do it."   That is a big factor in life, as well as bowling! Find a great coach and mentor to guide you.

  Bowling ball weight blocks: For the most part, when we look at the cores of bowling balls we see often that there is a semi - pancake shaped puck at the top of the weight block core.
    Or there may be a puck at the bottom of the core. You might even see one at the top and one at the bottom of the core.
    If you purchase a ball that has a puck at the bottom of the ball, most likely your ball reaction is going to be a smooth curve from your release back into the pin deck.
    However, if you purchase a ball and **the puck is at the top of the core you "should" get a "skid"- "snap" type of reaction from your ball. Again, as always, it's all about how you release the ball.**

  If you are a high rev player, you can spin anything! Surface and length of travel down the floor may be your focus. However if you are not a high rev bowler, then cores that are weighted "AWAY" from your finger tips and more towards the thumb are often a better choice in my opinion.

The object is to get the densest mass core weight "away" from your fingertips. Like a plastic coke bottle, you can place the base of the bottle between your thumb and fingers and try to flip it end-over-end. Yes it's awkward and a little difficult. *(A juggler does not juggle a bowling pin from the bottom.)* Next try flipping the bottle with the small end between your fingers and thumb. What a difference? Not only in the speed of the flip, but the control also!

*** With all bowling balls this is a general observation and ultimately the drilling of the ball, and the bowler who delivers the ball has the final say in what the ball does on the lane for them.

Bowling Balls that hook too much - To have a bowling ball that hooks **too much** is rare. **Let put it out there, today your ball thinks that all you want to do is just hit the 7 pin.** Let's face it, bowling balls are made to react and hook, that's what they are designed to do. Let's look at why it may not be the ball's fault that it is **hooking too much** for you!
  – Can the **lanes be very dry** today?
  – Can you be **too slow to the approach?**
  – Could you **not have enough ball tilt** in reference to the lane?
  – Can the **surface of the ball be too rough?**
  – Is the **ball falling off your hand too early?**
  – Are you on **a very short oil pattern today?**
  – If you wear a wrist brace, **are you dialed up for lots of hook?**
  – Do you normally stand **close up on the approach**?
  – Do you use less than **3 steps to deliver** the ball?
  – Do you have a very **slow swing** speed?
  – Is your swing speed good, but you break your wrist and ball inside **just prior to the point of delivery** losing speed to the pins.
  – Are you putting the ball down in the **dry heads** causing the pin to fall down early and the ball to **"roll out"** too soon?
  – Are you just using the **"wrong release"** for this condition today?

*** **Should you purchase the "Bowling Coach in a bag?"** - **It will help you** take a look at some of those items above when you are on the lanes practicing! www.TrueBowlerAdjustments.com

Ball tape - Black/white: The thickness of ball tape is the first thing that needs to be addressed. The black tape is 1/16th of and inch thick, and the **white tape is thicker** that's it!

If you use white tape on the padded side of your thumb from the right side of the hole back around to the left you can change your delivery angle by several boards. Just remember that if your shot keeps going to the left and your thumb feels okay, but you can wiggle it a bit more inside the hole you probably need to add a piece of tape to the right side of the thumb hole. Maybe even change the tape you may have in your ball **because it is worn out** from the last "15 games" you bowled with it.

Additionally, if you happen to go out to bowl and notice that your ball usually heads toward the right gutter way too soon in your delivery, and you just can't seem to hit your target which is to the left of where your ball keeps rolling; check your tape and its position in your ball. **Take it out if needed.** Placing white tape between your thumb and the fingers will firm up the span or feel on the pads of the fingers.

Caution here again – If you have **LATE TIMING** or you are trying to use **a spinning release**, your ball may fly out to the right also, so just be aware of these two factors when considering adding tape.

If you move the tape from the right side of the thumbhole to the left toward the middle finger you will engage it and the middle finger will become more communicative with the thumb and lesser with the ring finger. Often times providing less turn to the ring finger, but more lift to the middle finger moving the shot itself to finish more to the left.

Ball Tape (Black): Black tape is normally used on the backside of the thumbhole. Since it is so thin you should make a base for the black tape with the white tape, placing the black tape directly on a piece of white tape before inserting it in the hole. The reason for this is two fold.
 # 1 - Because the black tape is so thin you will probably need 3 to 4 pieces to make a good fit. **#2 -** If you have ever placed black tape in a ball against just the ball and no white tape under it, you know the headache of trying to scrape that tape off the sides of the hole after a few days of sitting inside the ball!

Combating Conditions
Ball Polishing (ball sanding) - Other than appearance, polishing a ball is meant to make the ball "skid" further down the lane before hooking and rolling towards the pins a well as making the surface tacky to grab the dry backend once it begins its exit out of the oil. Polish can come in different grits as mentioned on page 44.

You can **sand a ball** to grab the lane. The different sanding pads used, can take the cover of the bowling ball from **virtually slick like ice** down to nasty, gnarly, **scratchy, grit like,** to dig into the oil and **provides increased friction with the lanes. Sanding may widen the ball track creating more ball surface area like a tire grabbing the lane.**
These pads goes from 4000 grit (**Slick**) to 800 and 350 (**rough**) commercially, unless you checkout a few hardware stores to go lower.

It takes a little time to figure out what works. Sometimes sanding it down and then polishing it afterwards works well for a bowler.

See what works for you. Changing the surface is part of adjusting for any Truebowler. Even if it may not be recommended by the bowling ball company. **You are responsible for your bowling**. Especially when you are an **advanced bowler averaging 170-200+**. If you are not aware of bowling balls and how to adjust them for lane conditions, then it will be very difficult to attain consistency with pin carry. **Remember,** the next level after advanced bowler 200+ **is the PROFESSIONAL Level. You are almost there! Congrats!**

Scotch Brite pads and you!!!!

Scotch brite pads are the green or brown pads we use to clean dishes or other house ware items. Scotch brite pads can be used by hand to rough up the ball surface to provide friction for the ball and lane contact.

Caution has to be used that you don't apply too much pressure as you go over the surface of the ball evenly. Always keep in mind; **once you have dulled up your ball and it starts to "hook" you can not make it go back to being glossy to skid further during play. Especially, if you make the mistake of dulling it up too much just before league play. Ball Position: (Height)** – I have witnessed countless times where a bowler is dialed into a shot on the lanes and suddenly, the bowler loses the edge. Not necessarily because of lane conditions changing. Moreover, **the ball position has dropped considerably during play.**

Often the player will refocus and raise the ball too high, to compensate for being a little physically tired, and the string of missed attempts may continue.

One of the bugs in your delivery may be you have the ball too low in your delivery which allows you to move faster, but makes the ball finish higher in the pocket.

Otherwise, you have the ball a little too high in your starting position on the approach. You will notice in practice that your release "skids," "hooks," and "rolls" a lot further down the lane. This is absolutely fine to use as an adjustment if you are coming up high on the head pin.

Likewise, **if you are leaving 10 pins, drop your ball position a little, keep your speed up and follow through ensuring you roll over your target, to carry the 10 pin. This will reduce the revolutions on your ball if you are delivering end-over-end. (Never be too far away from the headpin!)**

Ball Height and Spare shots **- Countless times you will see other bowlers miss a pin on a drier shot to the left. Raising your ball height on spare shots will get you into the habit of finishing your spare shots and compensating for the dryness of the lanes at times. *Make this adjustment part of your routine if it is right for you!***

Hand Positions

Hand positions are such a mystery to bowlers. All you ever hear is: "change your hand position to make it hook sooner or the infamous **"roll"** the ball over your target."

One of the first questions from a backup bowler is always, "Now how do you want me to "hold" the ball before I "throw" it down the lane?" Ironically, backup bowlers hold the ball basically like everyone else. Let's just work with three ways to "hold" the ball so you can get the ball down the lane.

The first one is to hold the ball extended straight down by your side with the ball straight down beside you, turn your hand counter clockwise (right handed) so that your thumb is directly beside your leg and fingers are away from you to the outside gutter or channel. This is one position swing designed for beginners to allow them to turn their arms and body to deliver the ball onto the lane and **quickly move beyond negotiating the approach.**

Keep this position in the approach stance; maintain it through the push away, and the back swing. There is no rotation of the wrist even through release. The ball will go straight down the lane after a few attempts. Some bowlers will notice the rotation and hook of the ball only after several releases. **This position places the thumb to the left of the fingers** and not over top of them. This release position is called the Suitcase position. The wrist and finger position at release is **vertical** to the floor.

Vertical when you are holding the ball on the approach, **vertical** when you swing the ball in your backswing, **vertical** when you release the ball and come up to the 12 o'clock position above your head.

I mailed President Obama a copy of my book to get him jump-started after his one-hundred days in office. You may know his bowling outing during his campaign **did not** go so smooth. The illustration below shows the suitcase hand position at release. This position is **described as extending your hand as if you were going to shake hands with the pins** at the other end of the lane.

A bowler who enjoys bowling with family and friends occasionally should use this release. Once a week league nights are great for this release, however only in bowling centers where there is plenty of oil on the lanes, which allow the bowler to deliver a comfortable shot without having to really swing the ball with a lot of effort to get the ball down the lanes. I will try to write in the left-hander's voice.

Big O Concepts   *True Bowler Adjustments*

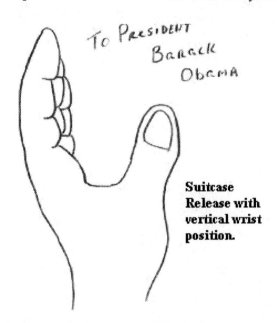

To PRESIDENT
BARACK
OBAMA

Suitcase Release with vertical wrist position.

Suitcase Release - The hand does not deviate from the position you see displayed. The hand and arm swings back to front until released exactly like the picture above. The follow through will finish above the head at the 12 o'clock position.

ART BY

Jenny
1 May 2009

Thanks for everything you are doing! - *TrueBowler*

Thumb over the top of the fingers is the preferred method of positioning, yet **negotiating the approach** with the **vertical wrist position release** is our goal.

*** A word of caution concerning **the suitcase release.** In my experience: Bowlers who have **overly used the suitcase release** (bowling twice a week, 6 to 10 games or more) often end up with **a shoulder injury.** Some damage to the rotator cuff or some other injury often occurs. Again, if you only bowl every now and then or very **infrequently**, there should be no problems using the suitcase release as long as you **are not** bowling this way regularly.

Please only use the suitcase release for a limited time until you can adequately negotiate the approach. Then, find a coach who can work with you to get your thumb above your fingers. With their help, you can swing, lift, or spin the ball into the lane, as it should be properly done.

The second position of release (**after negotiating the approach**) is to support the ball with your left hand and release the ball textbook style, which would be to turn your wrist with the thumb away from your body **counter-clockwise (lefty). This will place the thumb above the fingers in the stacked position.**

Big O Concepts   *True Bowler Adjustments*

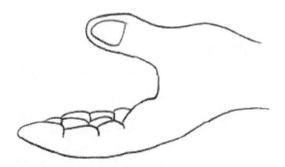

Second style of delivery uses a flat wrist position or a 45 degree obliqued wrist position. Still the object of the release is to deliver the ball with the thumb above the fingers.

May 2009

This position is so that your fingers are pointing more naturally down lane and so that your wrist is 45 degrees to the floor, and 45 degrees axis rotation to the lane at the release point. The thumb may be slightly tilted to the 11 o'clock position behind the ball, (left handed) or 1 o'clock position (right handed).

The third hand position is often the first hand position taught to bowlers. This position places your **wrist/hand in a flat position to the floor** for throwing a straight ball. The hand with fingers pointed down lane will only release the ball **(hopefully)** straight **end-over-end.** Concentrate on **lifting the hand and finger joints up the back of the ball. Spin** is often delegated to the pads of the fingers or fingertips. However, you should **not** to spin **the hand** to the outside of the ball. Placing the ball in the palm of the hand in the beginning of training often "in my humble opinion" engages the forearm and bicep muscles.

This early engagement leaves something special to be desired of coaches when they are asked to help a bowler to achieve a "free arm swing" after many years of bowling a particular way.

As bowlers become more accurate and experienced efforts to flatten the hand out and firm up the wrist for increase turn on the ball should be attempted, however, never forced. If it looks unnatural, chances are it is going to hurt in the long run. Always strive to **keep the thumb above the fingers at release** to allow the thumb to exit the ball prior to turning the ball. Although it is the preferred starting position for most instructors, naturally the next step is asking the student to curl their middle finger and ring finger in the ball to provide lift and spin to the ball.

Often this move or "feel" takes a few practice sessions to accomplish creating the revolutions on the ball that give the bowler more opportunities and strikes. This curling of the fingers, lifting and spinning the ball at release allows the ball to slow down after the mid-lane allowing the ball to rev up and make the run for the 5 pin.

Cupping your hand and wrist will aid in creating more lift for your release. Cupping the ball takes lots and lots of practice and /or wrist braces for us mortals to master because the wrist joint itself is freely movable.

****Hand positions affect axis rotation and axis tilt. Use your non-bowling hand to "set" your ball tilt and axis rotation prior to delivery!

Hand Releases: There are three positions of hand release at the deposal of a Truebowler. The first release is that of a spinner.

The thumb releases out of the ball in an "arrow release" (See illustration # 10), that is almost parallel to the floor. **It is not normally achieved this way but exceptions are seen. This is just** *"for example only to show you the spin of the ball."*

What is important here is **the spinning circle that is created at the bottom of the ball.** This is typical of a good release especially the 1 o'clock release. Again, this example is to just demonstrate that the ball will sit and spin on one point unless we swing it down lane.

True Bowler Adjustments.com

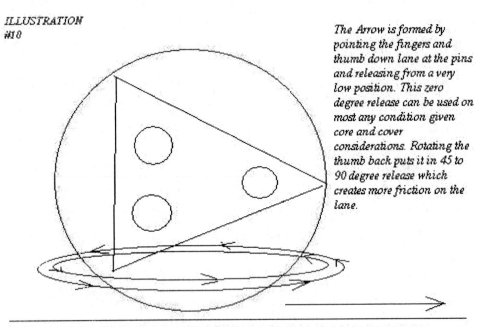

ILLUSTRATION #18

The Arrow is formed by pointing the fingers and thumb down lane at the pins and releasing from a very low position. This zero degree release can be used on most any condition given core and cover considerations. Rotating the thumb back puts it in 45 to 90 degree release which creates more friction on the lane.

SPINNING LOW TRACK - RELEASE JUST BEHIND THE SLIDING FOOT LEVEL TO THE LANE. COMBATS DRIER CONDITIONS. VERY READABLE TO THE POCKET.

This ball "spins" as you release it down the floor with very little contact with the floor and a low track, until almost midlane. Just like a spinning top, if you were to place the ball on the floor and spin it, it would stay in one spot and just turn. When you add the swing of the arm, you get forward motion. The release is accomplished just as the ball arrives at the back of the slide foot. At this point, the thumb is forward and along with the fingers, they are level or parallel to the floor. A moderate swing and spin are all that is required to deliver an adequate hooking ball.

* <u>NOTE:</u> This type of spinner is not the helicopter spinner where the delivery and release of the ball onto the lane is from the top of the ball. The arrow truly just tries illustrates the spin we try to achieve with the ball in an effort to create skid. This spinning skid helps in most deliveries.
Next is the "stroker" or 45 degrees hand release. This release is truly an individual achievement for those who use it. Like the spinner release the thumb is forward in the arrow position, however the position of the arrow is now release at 45 degrees to the floor with an inward and upward lift release, mostly **end-over-end**. This release can also be projected with a lot of side lift and turn to the left, while spinning the bottom of the ball.

Spinning the bottom of the ball with this release is done to consistently clear heads that are dry. **(See illustration # 11)**

TrueBowlerAdjustments.com

ILLUSTRATION #11

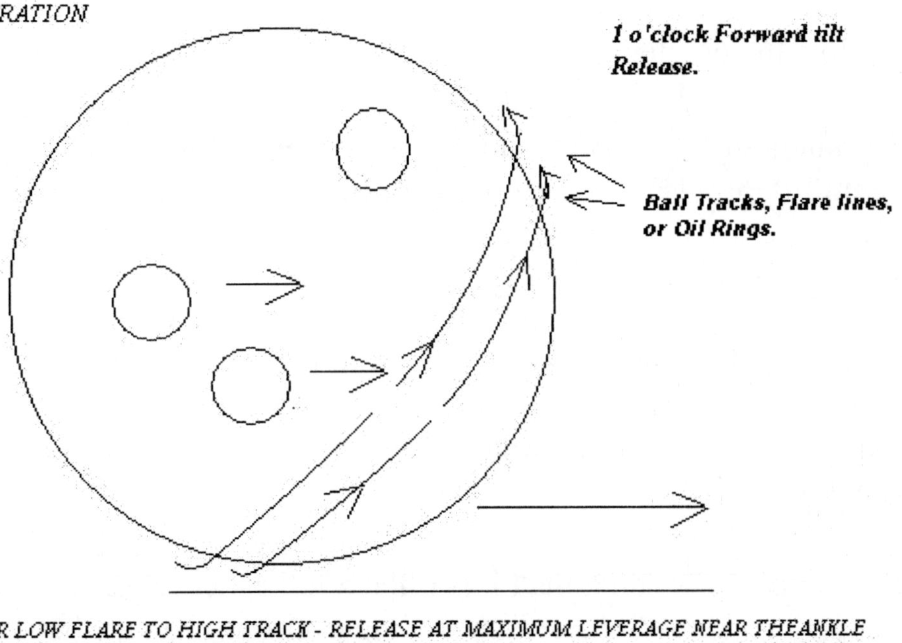

1 o'clock Forward tilt Release.

Ball Tracks, Flare lines, or Oil Rings.

STROKER LOW FLARE TO HIGH TRACK - RELEASE AT MAXIMUM LEVERAGE NEAR THE ANKLE OF THE SLIDE FOOT WITH FORWARD BALL TILT. READS THE LANE SOONER THAN SPINNING RELEASE FOR MEDIUM OILED LANES.

The lift that occurs at release follows through into the lane. This forward tilt or release can be used when you have too much oil for a lower style spinning release, and you need the ball to read the backend sooner.

Having only one way to deliver the ball can be counter productive in at least one game of play. Especially, when a house condition becomes wet/dry at the back end and you only have two bowling balls. A rash of splits will signal this condition. This truly is the time to be versatile in your delivery and **try a different release, or a use a more stable rolling ball.**

STACKED RELEASE, or maximum 90 degree side roll, that places your hand on the back of the ball, turning to the side of the ball in an effort to rip the cover off of it as they say. Delivering the ball off both fingers together is the way to start out. **What is most important here is keeping the thumb directly above the fingers.** Spinning the ball to three o'clock and no more. **Much like a spinning top from above the ball looking down when you deliver the ball onto the lane, this "creates skid" and saves revolutions for the backend.**

Recognizing **non-reaction** with your **end-over-end** release may be simply remedied by changing your delivery. Rotating your hand **to the side** of the ball in a **stacked release allows you to spin the ball** in an effort to create skid on the front end. **Just like the end-over-end release** your can start your spin from the 6o'clock, 5o'clock or from the 3o'clock positions.

Lastly, minor adjustments should be **"practiced before play"** include: using **the middle finger**, and then **use the ring finger** at release and see what it does separately for you from one shot to the other. Often employing the **middle finger** will make the ball grab early or roll out early (turn). Using the **ring finger** will increase the distance of travel when using more of a behind the ball delivery, push and forward roll somewhat is achieved. Still, when using the ring finger the **thumb is above the fingers** with the slightest of side turn of the ball. Sometimes this same release is referred to as **"bellying the ball."**

When I see someone doing that, it is often a full roller release. They have passed the 3 o'clock position, and are pulling backwards on the ball somewhat at release. **(See illustration # 12)**

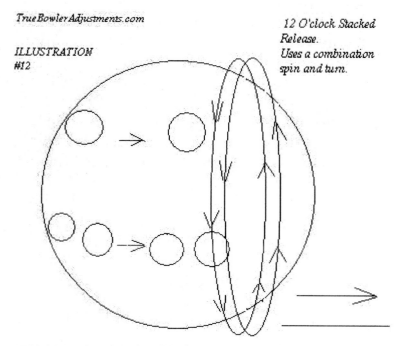

TrueBowlerAdjustments.com

*ILLUSTRATION
#12*

*12 O'clock Stacked
Release.
Uses a combination
spin and turn.*

*STACKED 12 O'CLOCK RELEASE - HELD IN THE BEGINNING APPROACH
STANCE FROM THE BACK OF THE BALL.
*DURING THE LAST 1/4 OF THE SWING NEAR THE ANKLE, THE HAND ROTATES
FROM 6 O'CLOCK TO 3 O'CLOCK TO THE SIDE OF THE BALL AT RELEASE,
SPINNING, LIFTING, AND ROLLING THE BALL ONTO THE LANE AT RELEASE.*

In the stacked release, the objective is to attack the lanes with maximum side roll and flare without hitting up on the ball. I will ask this question: Have you ever seen bowlers walking around practicing the hand twist in the air? Most of them are practicing some variation of the wrist/hand rotational motion that is used by bowlers during their releases. Therefore, whether the release is spinning, end-over-end, or a stacked cranker release, you would do well to practice with and without the ball to get your release together.

End-Over-End Release - The end-over-end release is fairly straightforward. Your can vary your delivery. Your can hold the ball in the stacked release from behind, or at 45 degrees behind or 5 o'clock behind the ball or with the thumb somewhat on the in the 1 o'clock position from behind the ball. Generally only turning the ball ¼ of a turn and flipping the ball off your finger pads.

With the finger pads or tips of your fingers, simply lift with both fingers and eject the thumb out of the ball in a forward roll as you project your shot down lane. Only spin the ball forward.

63   **www.TrueBowlerAdjustments.com**

Most bowlers will project the ball off of there finger tips as the ball just passes the ankle or the bowler may release the ball just a bit out in front of the ankle.

There is no spinning of the ball at the bottom most times, or to the outside of the ball. **Lateral spinning** would imply circling your fingers to the outside of the ball either from middle or at the bottom of the ball. Keep in mind to just come up the back of the ball and have your finger tips curled back towards your thumb at release.

TrueBowlerAdjustments.com

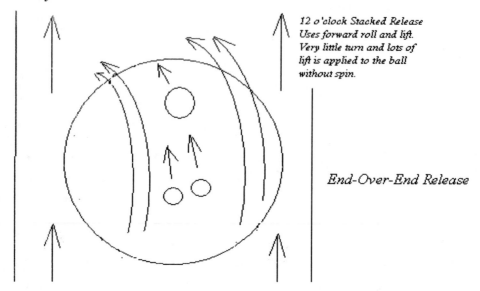

12 o'clock Stacked Release Uses forward roll and lift. Very little turn and lots of lift is applied to the ball without spin.

End-Over-End Release

STACKED 12 O'CLOCK RELEASE - HELD IN THE BEGINNING APPROACH STANCE FROM THE BACK OF THE BALL.
DELIVERED FROM THE 6 o'clock TO THE 12 OR 1 O'CLOCK POSITION CONQUERS MANY HOUSE SHOTS AND PROVIDES MANY GOOD LAYOUT OPTIONS.

Arguably, the simple end-over-end will defeat **85%** of the house shots and tournaments shots. It often has a smoother and extremely readable ball path to the pins. As, people say, "straighter is greater!" It's just not really fancy, for most people who participate in modern bowling. **Regardless of the delivery you choose, it just has to be repeatable!**

Again, if you place your hand to the back of the ball or under the ball and come straight up the back of the ball with **the thumb above the fingers** or tilted to the right slightly, still in the 1 o'clock position, you can come from behind or under the ball and deliver an **END-OVER-END** shot down lane. Do not allow your hand to circle the ball to the outside. This will turn or spin the ball! You do not want to spin the ball in high oil, most often it will go in the channel or gutter.

Often times the **end-over-end** may require you to open up your **shoulder** to release a good shot and to get good length down the lane. Again, remember to keep **the thumb above the fingers** and come from under and behind the ball **without** turning to the side of the ball. Extending and splitting your index finger may help to remind you not to spin the ball to the side. Your follow through should be straight up to the 12 o'clock or 1 o'clock position Still you can deliver **three end-over-end releases.** (Starting from 6o'clock, from 5o'clock and from the 3o'clock positions which is more of a side roll.)

Lastly, I see the cranker style of setup and release when out on the lanes. The set up of placing the hand behind the ball with the fingers downward to 7 o'clock and the thumb at 1 o'clock gives the ball an awful lot of gitty up when released expertly. **(See illustration # 13)**

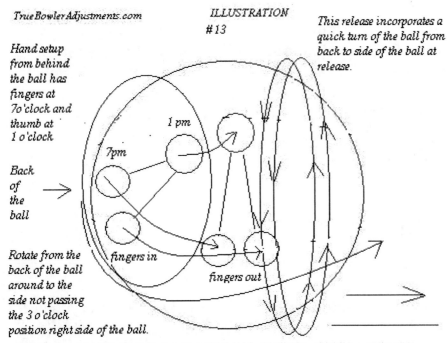

TrueBowlerAdjustments.com

ILLUSTRATION #13

This release incorporates a quick turn of the ball from back to side of the ball at release.

Hand setup from behind the ball has fingers at 7o'clock and thumb at 1 o'clock

Back of the ball →

Rotate from the back of the ball around to the side not passing the 3 o'clock position right side of the ball.

1 pm

7pm

fingers in

fingers out

STACKED 12 O'CLOCK RELEASE - HELD IN THE BEGINNING APPROACH STANCE FROM THE BACK OF THE BALL. 7PM / 1PM SETUP IN THE STANCE *DURING THE LAST 1/4 OF THE SWING NEAR THE ANKLE, THE HAND ROTATES FROM 7 O'CLOCK TO 3 O'CLOCK TO THE SIDE OF THE BALL AT RELEASE, SPINNING, LIFTING, AND ROLLING THE BALL ONTO THE LANE AT RELEASE.

Advanced to Professional Bowler

Adjustments 170 – 200+ average

THE LANE

Lane Reading - Most bowlers hope the same thing when they are standing on the approach. Mainly that the lanes are oiled "just for them that day." Not too wet, and not too dry.

You know how you are going to release the ball onto the lanes, and you know body adjustments you will make. You selected the bowling balls to help get you to the pocket. You have the correct fit, weight and different ball covers. **What we find when we get on the approach is that the lanes either have way to much oil for us, or that the lane is hooking a little bit too much**, (maybe kind of on the dry side) yet it may seem okay - **for the moment!**

The most important thing for you as a top-level bowler at this point is to always know what is length of the lane oil is for any shot you bowl on from this point on. Always ask, inquire or research what the lane condition is will be like before bowling so you can be more informed about the pattern you are bowling on. Make a simple phone call. Sometimes you can simply ask the lane mechanic. Sometimes the tournament director or official will have this information or you can down load it from the internet prior to participating. Someone knows the lane condition and so should you!!!

Dry Lane Conditions

Lane Reading **"UNCONVENTIONAL"**

Let's tackle **the drier lane conditions** - To understand the dry lane you need a visual image of what is in front of you. Truebowler looks at the "hooking" oil pattern as a reverse arch, or as the old schoolers call it the reverse Christmas tree pattern. It's easy to identify with this pattern by simply thinking of the lane and the backend, as having **a circle** drawn in front of the head pin. (See illustration # 14)

This circle extends from one side of the lane to the other, gutter to gutter.

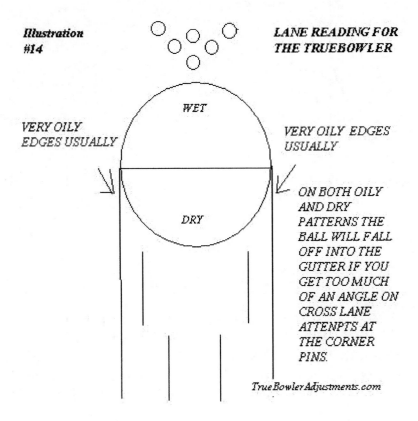

Illustration #14

LANE READING FOR THE TRUEBOWLER

WET

VERY OILY EDGES USUALLY

VERY OILY EDGES USUALLY

ON BOTH OILY AND DRY PATTERNS THE BALL WILL FALL OFF INTO THE GUTTER IF YOU GET TOO MUCH OF AN ANGLE ON CROSS LANE ATTENPTS AT THE CORNER PINS.

DRY

True Bowler Adjustments.com

The circle itself represents where the ball will peal off and head back to the pins. We call this circle **the break point** for the ball.

Your focus should be to imagine there is a circle down lane, or a line where your ball comes off its intended ball path down lane and heads back to the middle towards the headpin.

Now imagine the top half of the circle closest to the head pin is not there.

(See illustration #15 on the next page)

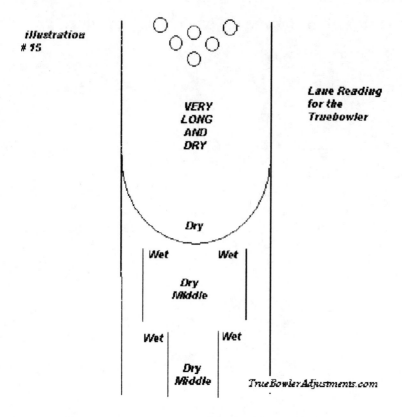

Now as you can see, the distance from the bottom-center edge of the circle is very far away from the head pin. This bottom circle is your dryer imagined **break point half circle** where your ball will hook and head back to the head pin!

This "**reverse arch**" for the dry shot end of the oil pattern has a half circle (or break point area) that is toward you, kind of like drawing a smile on the end of the oil pattern where it dips in the middle back toward you.

When bowling the reverse arch pattern with the bottom half of the circle pointed towards you, you will find that there is very little oil in the middle, often times your ball rolls nicely if you are playing the track, laying down around the 10 board and skidding to mid lane with no problems and then .... **hold on!**

Why does my ball keep hooking **into the head pin?** It's because the part of the reverse arch that **your ball is reading is crossing the bottom edge of the circle too soon. It has been said they don't use the reverse pattern any more however, "the middle can really be <u>that</u> dry!"**

You may try to move left as we are all taught to move "into the oil," however, if your ball drives into the **nose of the pins even more** or goes "Brooklyn" or to the left of the head pin. That is because you may now be throwing directly into the dry middle of the lane. Or hopefully you didn't move onto the 10 board that is probably dry from everyone else playing there before you adjusted there. You would have to figure at this point a True Bowler is going to use whatever works to score. **So you try to adjust!**

You move to the right just a little further outside the 10 board, and the most incredible thing happens,... I'll be a monkey's uncle! That darn ball just kept going down the lane to the outside and took out the three pin and made a hole in the pins leaving the 10 pin, as if it was so oily on the outsides the ball could not hook at all. Did you spin the ball?

This reverse arch **has oil on the outside** down the lane where it seems that past the 10 board is **out of bounds** (sometimes referred to as **"OOB"**), and the ball won't come back to the pins. Often times to get the length down the lane to the pocket you have to attack this shot or oil pattern by figuring a way to go off the corners of the arch and getting your distance down the lane, which may mean "sometimes" throwing straight up the 6th/7th and 8th boards. **Remember, it's not good to spin the ball when there is high or heavy oil!**

Also, if you are playing the track area to get more length out of the ball, moving to the middle with **a high pinned polished ball and a light core** where the lane is much drier, yet it may be a more even shot in the middle. It may allow you to play there just as long as you don't get too far right of the 15 board, back to the 10 board. **Knowing which release to use is crucial.**

Just try to smooth curve the ball right up the middle out to and over the 15 board and back to the pins. We have a lot of old school bowlers who will still move left over to 25/30/35 to find the oil to get down the lane. Knowing that the ball is hooking in the middle, it makes good sense that once you cross over that dry area with your feet, to the left, you'll get back into the oil around 25 to 30 left, just above the foul line. Again, **are you end-over-end with your release, or are you spinning the ball at release?**

Dry Center of the Lane: The problem when you go left and deliver the ball is that you may inadvertently set the ball down between the 25 left and the 15 board which **may be the dry area in the center of the lane!** Thus, making the ball hook again before getting to the backend. Setting the ball down in oil on the 25 to the 30-board side and rolling across the dry middle towards your target should be the preferred angle of attack.

This area around 25/35 board can enhance scores, however the lay down has to be just a little past the foul line about 6 inches to 1 foot if that much into the heads. Since there is oil from the 15 board back to the 10 board on both sides, putting the ball down early on the left will allow the ball to land in oil saving energy and revolutions as it crosses the dry into the mid lane and begins to read. (Tweeners/crankers will love this tip!)

Shooting 10 Pins and 7 Pins - Flatting the hand out (Corner Pins)

Your forearm, wrist and hand are parallel to the floor with the palm facing up to the ceiling. This will place your thumb and fingers pointing up to the ceiling also. For some bowlers who really spin the ball to get revs on the shot, this position can caused bowlers to hit up on the ball at release causing inconsistencies. If this happens to you, try the follow changes:

While maintaining **the flattened out hand and wrist, I recommend that you rotate your hand counter clockwise until the tips of the fingers are parallel with the floor instead of pointing up at the ceiling.** This maneuver also places the thumb more parallel across the body. (**once again, the thumb is above the fingers**) This helps gives the ball **more forward roll** much like the straight ball. When delivering from the left side of the lane to the right, **the axis rotation of the ball will be basically at zero** when the ball lands on the lane, as long as you **turn your body and face your target** and the pin you are trying to hit. Bowlers can also try to lead with the ring finger at 10 pins.

Bowlers can **also try breaking the wrist downward just a bit.** Remember to firm the wrist and hand back up to support the ball at release. Depending on the angle of your wrist, you may be able to decrease your axis rotation to almost zero depending on how true you are facing the corner pin that gives you the most trouble. Your palm may even be facing the pin depending on how much you direct the ball and reduce your axis rotation. Not only is this great for shooting 10 pins, **bowlers may be able to increase the skid on his ball with that hand position when the ball is coming in too high on the head pin at times.** Sometimes lowering the ball helps with a good delivery to the corner pins also. Oddly enough, bowlers who are opposite eye dominant players, my find corner pins to be their most challenging spares. This spare will take a particular mindset and lots of practice.

Shooting at 10 pins: Since there is normally some oil is from 15 to 10, you may find that you are most accurate aligning your target between the 15 board and the 10 board. You should use a low ball tilt towards the 10 pin, low axis rotation or a straighter ball release. Right-handed bowler leads with the ring finger to the 10 pin. **(shorter finger at the high numbered pin)**

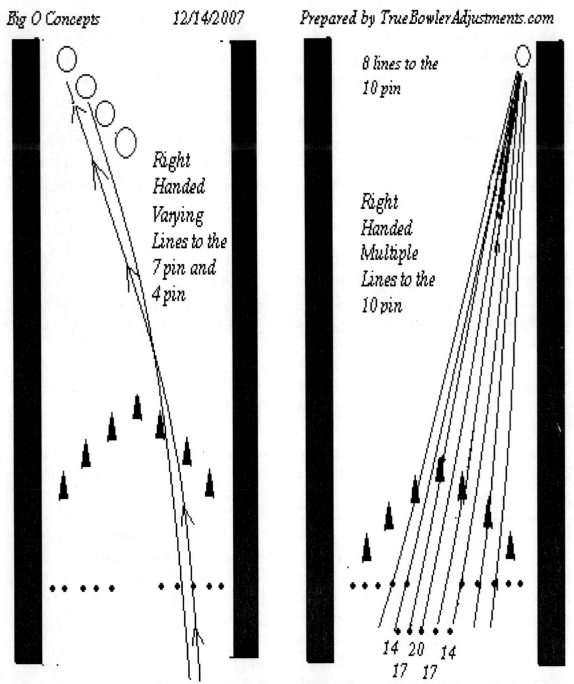

Big O Concepts

Big O Concepts   *12/14/2007*   *Prepared by TrueBowlerAdjustments.com*

Right Handed Varying Lines to the 7 pin and 4 pin

8 lines to the 10 pin

Right Handed Multiple Lines to the 10 pin

14   20   14
17   17

Each of the middle targets are 3 boards apart

1 - The most success can be achieved by targeting the 4th dot on the left and the 5th arrow. **2** - Also, you can target the 5th dot on the left and in between the 5th and 4th arrows. **3** - Lastly, you can target the 5th dot over the middle arrow depending if the lanes are dry on the backend, or you have some surface on your bowling ball, always deliver any attempt at the 10 pin **with good timing at release. Players who want to throw the 3rd arrow on the right may be best served by playing the 17/16 board at the dots, over the third arrow. Ball Recommendation:** Columbia White dot and the Ebonite Maxim plastic spare balls.

As an additional tip! If you take a moment to look at the 5 dots to the right of the lane just past the foul line going out to the arrows, you will notice that **the 5th dot lines directly up with your beloved 10 pin!!!** Isn't that amazing?!!!!

Go ahead, set the ball down early and roll over the dot, between the 2nd and 3rd arrows right to the 10 pin!!! Again, bowlers with good speed and revolution at release will find the 15 or 17 board to be a good target near the 3rd arrow to the 10 pin. Remember the preferred release is **End-over-End.** Do not spin the ball at delivery **unless the conditions allow it.**

Where to Stand? Recommendation from TrueBowler – Stand far <u>right</u> and <u>back</u> for your 7 pin (right handers) This will give you more time to align and walk to your targets. As you move to the left, you should <u>move up closer to the front set of approach dots or in front of them</u> for the 10 pin as you get to the left side of the lane.

AGAIN, you may have to **move farther up on the approach, for your 10 pin right handers**, and **up for your 7 pin left handers.**

You may have to move **back for your 7 pin or 4 pin right-handers** and **back for your 10 pin left-handers.** This gives you more room to acquire your targets as you approach the lane.

The majority of bowlers will find that they **definitely can use the targets** however, because of their **individual height and body styles** they do not have to step as far back on the approach. Some bowlers will use the 4th dot as a reference or the 3rd dot only. **Because of vision issues,** they may just look through these targets just to acquire the range finders at the back of the lane near the pins. In any event, **these are sound targets** in any respect.
The overall goal for you as the bowler should be for you to **pick out at least two or three lines to the 7 pin** and **then pick out two or three lines to the 10 pin.** ONE LINE IS FOR **OILY LANES** and the other lines are for **DRIER LANES** especially if you should decide not to use a plastic spare ball. **GET A SPARE BALL !!!**

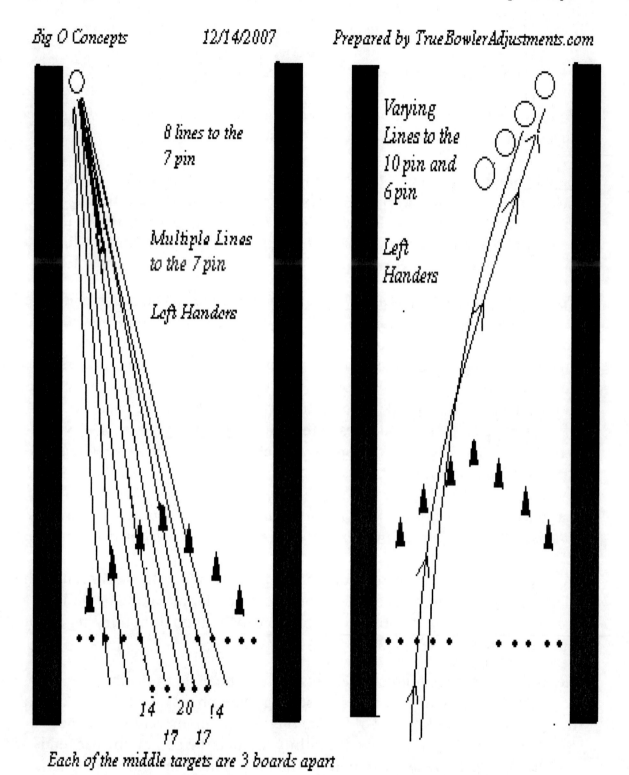

8 lines to the 7 pin

Multiple Lines to the 7 pin

Left Handers

Varying Lines to the 10 pin and 6 pin

Left Handers

14   20   14

17   17

Each of the middle targets are 3 boards apart

Once again, try stepping to the far left and up for your 10 pins.
Lefty – Step far right and up for 7 pins,

Righty- stepping back and to the right for your 7 or 4 pin conversions.

Lefty – step back and to the left for your 10 or 6 pin conversions.

Every coach has a pet peeve. "Don't have late timing!"

Follow *the recommendations* for where to stand, and *throw the designated targets* on the illustrations and you will score!

<u>**Left handed**</u> **bowlers can try the mapped out shots above. Remember to cater the shot to you. Left handed bowlers can lead with their ring fingers to shoot the 7 pin and with their middle finger to shoot the 10 pin if it helps. (shortest finger to the lowest number corner pin) (longest finger to the highest numbered corner pin)**

<u>**Final Note about 10 pins and 7pins:**</u> If you are really that accurate no one needs to tell you how to pick up pins. However, if you are someone who can connect the middle arrow to the last range finder to the 10 pin or to the 7 pin this shot may be better suited for you. (Provided you have range finders at your local bowling center.) Knowing that you can move inside on oily lanes to play the corner pins and move outside when it's dry on the backend will often save you a lot of headaches in the future. <u>**Remember** </u>**which way you will move <u>when it's wet</u>. <u>Remember</u> which way you will move <u>when it's dry</u> on the backend!**

Lane Reading (Wet lanes) – *A bowler will never fully appreciate bowling on a house shot unless they have bowled on a heavy oiled tournament condition!*

Wet lanes - The "arch" pattern or long oil pattern, sometimes referred to the Christmas tree pattern. Recently a long time bowler and a man who is a true bowler said that he observed a phenomena that got him thinking about bowling in today's society.

He said, a tournament director was just telling the plain truth when he addressed the issue of oily lanes by stating; "members love to bowl, of that there is no doubt. However, if it is an oily competitive event where the average member does not have the ability to hook the ball on the backends, nor the skill **or knowledge** to deliver the ball to the head pin repeatedly, adjusting their body or the ball **…. the members will not participate!"**

This is the problem **high volume oil presents to bowlers in general.** High volume oil/long oil takes consistency and good accuracy to score.

When your house present long oil to you, now think of the end of the pattern as being the top of a circle away from you. This top of the circle is your **new break point area**. **(See illustration # 16)**

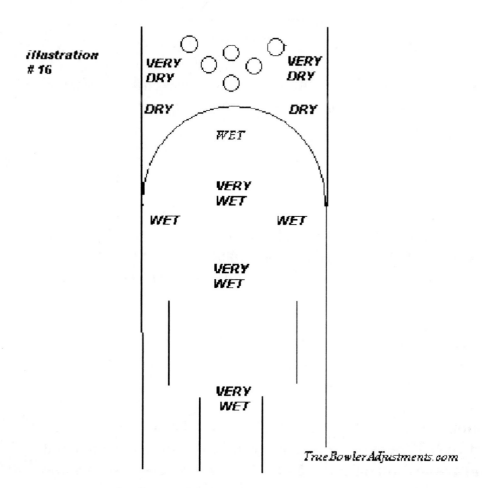

illustration # 16

TrueBowlerAdjustments.com

Also, think of the half circle end away from you and ending about 10 feet or 5 feet away from the head pin. Now imagine the middle of the lane has "lots of oil." You have no problem getting to the head pin. Unlike the dry middle of the reverse arch pattern. With that oil in the middle you can feel free to roll your non-reactive or spare ball, from left to right across the middle arrow to the 10 pin now and pick it up, without worry (Just remember Truebowler said **spare ball!!!).**

Likewise, you can use your spare ball to the left over the middle arrow. That was the easy part about the arch pattern or oily lane. Now the fun begins!

Scenario: You are on the approach and you have tried everything to get your ball to hook, but it won't. You miss single pin spares to the right or left because you are trying to bowl normal and time the hook to cover the pin you want to hit it but you barely touch it, if you hit it at all.

Lane Transition – Carry down is the action of **bowling balls rolling through the oil on the front part of the lane and depositing it along the surface of the lane to the back end of the lane.** Often times after half a game or so this build up of oil will be consolidated in front of the **3 pin and the 6 pin** for right handed bowlers. With a five man team (10 people) carry down could affect your shot just after the first frame of the first game causing your bowling ball not to react on the backend. **The lane-transitioning phase - will go from wet on the front end and dry on the backend,** *to drier on the front end and wetter on the backend,* *to dry on the front end, dry in the middle and dry on the backend.*

For your ball to read, **you need your ball to do something special.**

You have to make sure you cover the pin you are after, and you want the ball to be spinning or have enough revolutions on it at the pin deck that it just walks through the pins. Basically, a ball that does not read the backends tells you it's not the ball for that condition. It needs to be snapping through the pocket at the very backend.

For this to happen **you need surface** on your ball (rough sanding **as low as** 180 grit (Scotchbrite) - (plus) with a slow ball you need revolutions or spin. **Lots of oil will slow your ball down.**

An illustration of (oil) carry down is provided on the next page. With the exception of a reverse pattern, most patterns will get small to large amounts of carry down **near the 3 pin and the 6 pin. How soon carry down** shows up **to help you** or mostly **hinder you**, depends on the number of players participating, and the units of oil used on the pattern, along with what type of bowling balls are being used. For many the carry down is a welcome site because their balls finally can get to the headpin when it was so very dry before during the first game. For others they begin to leave bucket 2/4/5's or miss the head pin repeatedly. These bowlers need a bowling ball where the pin will drop and rev up just a little sooner!

Carry Down Illustration

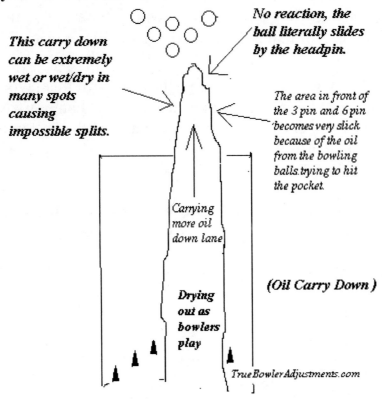

This carry down can be extremely wet or wet/dry in many spots causing impossible splits.

No reaction, the ball literally slides by the headpin.

The area in front of the 3 pin and 6 pin becomes very slick because of the oil from the bowling balls trying to hit the pocket.

Carrying more oil down lane

(Oil Carry Down)

Drying out as bowlers play

TrueBowlerAdjustments.com

To get the release position of the 1 o'clock arrow, your thumb/finger relation needs to be so that you can deliver the ball consistently towards the head pins directly, without being too slow and allowing the ball to go Brooklyn.

Because of the long oil and basically no reaction on the backend at the pocket, bowlers pound away with what would be a thundering crash of pins only to end up with a 5 pin leave or a 5/10 pin leave. Most often a 7 pin may accompany those two if you happen to be lucky enough to be leaving single pins. These balls are skidding and hooking **with no traction**.

It can get worst. You get frustrated and begin to leave the bucket 2/4/5 or worst yet you forget to be accurate and blow by the head pin and you are back to square one, missing the head pin and getting, no reaction.

Often a ball will stop reacting in the oil because of its layout, carry down and too little surface to lane contact. **Lofting the ball comes into play also as the heads begin to dry out.** This, delays the revving up process until the ball reaches the backend also. Ensure you have good speed at release when lofting the ball. A continuous curving layout is often a ball that is pinned above the fingers and below the fingers. The CG is often place in a direct line downward from the pin on the right side of the thumb. This continuous drill or strong curve drill is seen on many bowling balls in the bowling centers. Use the **incorrect release** with this drill in high oil, and the ball will not recover.

As mentioned earlier you may have to loft the ball with this layout to get it to react after carry down or in high oil. Sometimes changing your hand position from under the ball to higher on the back of the ball will create and earlier roll and cause the ball to hook before the carry down can affect the ball's hook to the pocket.

Although the following layout does well in the beginning on most lane conditions, You may loose hit at the pins as carry down increases often when using a spinning release.
(See illustration #17)

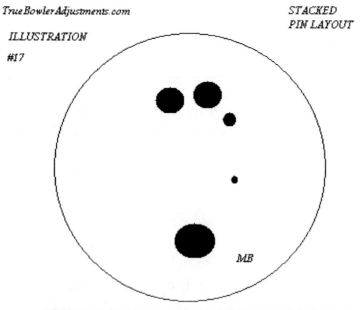

TrueBowlerAdjustments.com

ILLUSTRATION

#17

STACKED
PIN LAYOUT

MB

GENERALLY DISCRIBED AS THE STRONGEST LAYOUT FOR A BOWLER WHO HAS LOTS OF HAND REVOLUTIONS AND BALL SPEED. PROVIDES AWSOME RECOVERY FOR CRANKERS AND TWEENERS. STROKERS WHO MASTER BALL TILT CAN SCORE WELL PROVIDED THEY CAN DELAY THE HOOKING ACTION

With long oil patterns, **the preferred pin position** may be high above the fingers and closer out towards **your vertical axis line** or VAL. This line extends from the bottom of the ball through your PAP to the top of the ball. It parallels you grip line which runs from the bottom of your ball through the thumb between the fingers to the top of the ball.

This will get the most violent turn and the backend. Those who have good hand rotation can move outside a bit and play off the drier edge making parallel inside moves to stay in the pocket if the carry down starts to leave 10 pins. Those who normally go up the 10/12 board to reach corner shots may find that they are hooking and not able to convert shots like the 3/6/10. Instead, they take out just the 3 pin, or if the 4/7 was missed, it was because of the dry edges.

Truebowler highly recommends a harder cover, no core, spare ball for all occasions. Those in the game know that if you are converting your spares it will be much better than a 140 to 160 game.

When combating oil, **a spare ball** is a good weapon to use rolling at the "head pin" also for your strike ball. "Head pin," is the key point of interest not the pocket, as we would love to deliver the ball there.

Lane Reading (sport shot the ultimate oil condition) When you think of the sport shot the entire mindset has to adjust to the business at hand. In short, <u>everything</u> **becomes important.**

It's as if someone put a sheet of ice on the lane and said to you, "I'll give you a million dollars if you can throw 6 strikes in a row!" Truebowler knows to do that you have to know what position your arms are in, where your feet are on the approach, when you will be releasing your ball in your swing, how far into your delivery will you apply rotation to the ball, and where on the lane the ball will land. Will it land one foot, two feet, or out to three feet on the lane, and what release you are using.

Sport Shot - are you up against physics? Sport bowling requires you to be more technical in your delivery and your approach. Combined with the oily conditions a bowler now has to take into account that even though they are facing their target and walking towards it, the bowler themselves are moving in two distinct directions now. This is evident by releasing a perfect release at a near target only to see it go behind the pin you were aiming at. The end-over-end release may be your best friend.

Replay: You have lined up to hit the pocket from the right side. You deliver 3 shots and each of them at an angle, your shots hits way behind the head pin. Tossing from the 5 board to the pocket where you can clearly "see" the pocket is your worst shot. Are you spinning the release???

You take out the 3 pin and leave **1/4/7.** Why? The why is because your attack direction is magnified on a sport shot. You are moving towards your target in two directions. #1 you are moving to your left to head into the pocket. #2 you are moving forward on the lane. With so much oil, you are moving more forward faster to the back of the lane, than you are moving to your left. You need the correct release and the correct cover on your ball!

To conquer heavy oil, you must create surface on your ball.

Also, on your <u>normal house shot, most balls are label drill, or leverage drilled for skid/snap reaction.</u> I would like to say the majority of our bowlers are not speed demons. They are moderate to slow on the approach. Sport shots will require you to **use a ball that is more controlled and even rolling.** The pin will often be between, above, or below your fingers, in the middle of your span, or lastly, very close to your PAP. This will create a more stable roll to the pins.

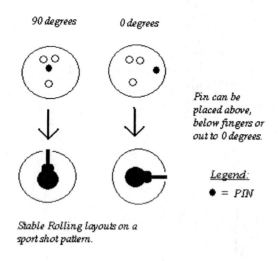

90 degrees   *0 degrees*

Pin can be placed above, below fingers or out to 0 degrees.

<u>*Legend:*</u>
● *= PIN*

Stable Rolling layouts on a sport shot pattern.

The Slant Shot - the forgotten straight shot. Since you are moving forward faster than you are moving to your left, separation occurs on the lane from your intended ball path to a point 2 to 4 inches behind or beyond where you wanted the ball to hit. Therefore, instead of your ball arriving to the side of the head pin and covering 3/4 of it, it arrives at the back of it slicing it out to the left or missing it completely to the right. Especially, if you are spinning the ball at release.

Make your target for sport shots an arrow to **a point at the front of the pin you are trying to hit,** if you are attempting angled shots. If you are using an unstable wrist position such as 45 degrees, you may be very inconsistent at spinning the ball in high oil. So much so, that if you use the arrows for targeting. Ensure you throw directly at the intended pin, whether you aim at the 1st, 2nd, or 3rd arrow. Use an **End-over-End Release!**

One of the first shots you learn in bowling is a straight shot. You should also learn its sister shot: **the slant shot.**

After bowling for months or years, we often times forget that we all generally started out throwing straight. A variation of straight is the slant shot.

There is no trying to hook the ball if you get no reaction on the **backend after numerous practice attempts with your highest hooking ball.** Even if you have changed hand positions to get maximum hook.

By this time, you will realize your ball is just not dull enough. In time, the pattern may dry out enough that you will get some reaction. Until then, throw the slant shot, cover the front of the pin on angled shots and pick up your spares if you leave anything. Using high revving ball with a small core is an option for strikes, and using a large core ball for spares will work if you like to use one ball for everything, since there is lots of oil. However, get a plastic spare ball.

What works best sometimes is to get a ball that will **"flip"** into the pocket or **arc,** at the backend. **The following illustration is a layout drill that should be in everyone's arsenal.**

Flip Drilling - Use this drilling in high oil and when there is lots of **carry down oil** in front of the pocket. Carry down occurs in front of the three pin for right-handed players, or the two pin for left-handed players. **The unique thing about a flip drill ball is that it truly is for the slow bowlers.** It revs very late, skidding through the front end picking up in the mid lane. You will see the ball on every turn, and then it picks up revs with lane travel. **On a sport shot, this ball can be very squirty (undesirable) on the backend.** With good speed and consistent shot delivery, you can score well even though it's not the preferred layout of choice. Remember that every bowling ball is unique to the person who throws it. **A variation** of the end-over-end release may be your ticket to success!

(Illustration #18 shows the Flip Drill Layout.)

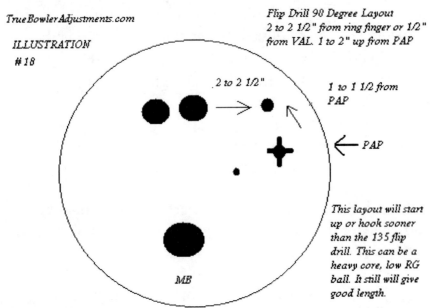

TrueBowlerAdjustments.com

*ILLUSTRATION
#18*

*Flip Drill 90 Degree Layout
2 to 2 1/2" from ring finger or 1/2"
from VAL. 1 to 2" up from PAP*

2 to 2 1/2"

*1 to 1 1/2 from
PAP*

PAP

*This layout will start
up or hook sooner
than the 135 flip
drill. This can be a
heavy core, low RG
ball. It still will give
good length.*

MB

*Flip Drill 90 Degree Layout - This ball has a delayed revving potential with an extremely late
break point. When delivered it will skid farther past mid lane and rev up immediately when it
encounters friction on the outside area or the backend. When lanes have initial carry down
transition or the long oiled condition exist, this is the layout to go to. With this ball you can
throw more inside and direct in oil, as well as closer to the outside lines when its dry. This is a
very versital layout for strokers. This layout often makes a very good first reactive ball layout.*

Special Note: Often times when the lanes are **very wet.** You may be able to
create an earlier roll by setting your ball down on the approach prior to the
foul line. **You will note that this does not set off the foul lights.**

This will provide hold after your release toward your intended target. Also,
as an added adjustment you can **roll your hand from under the ball**,
(reposition your hand by bringing the thumb up to the top of the ball.
Position your thumb to point across the lane, or just remember to start out
with your thumb level to the floor. **This position is to create earlier roll for
the ball right out of your swing.**

Dry Lanes: The following layout is a **Hook-N-Set type layout.** I see many
bowlers use this layout on drier lanes. The explanation can be a little
technical. However, the benefits are worth it.

When the lanes are dry, backend reaction is not a problem. However, **getting far enough down the lanes before the ball burns up is a problem.**

Getting out of the dry heads cleanly can also be a problem. Use a layout that is pinned near the PAP. Use a mass bias that is near the thumb preferably around **the 70 to 90 degree area**, this will **delay the revs** quite a bit with a slow controlled release. High grit polish around 2000 to 4000 will create more length.

Using an inside core that is not tall going up the pin, but one that is horizontal in profile 90 degrees to the pin, will give a higher RG effect for good carry and a quick roll out for the spot you are targeting.

(Hook and Set layout See illustration #19)

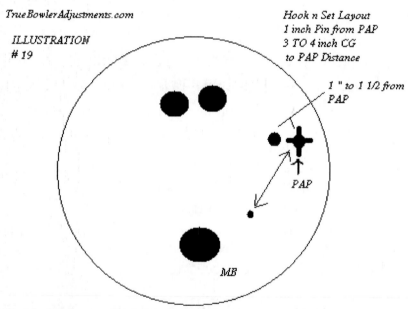

Hook and Set layout - This ball has a delayed revving potential with an early reading mid lane break point. When delivered it will skid and rev up just out of the heads and hook quickly. Once it has spun out into an early forward roll it will consistently deliver its punch into the pins until carry down weakens its strike potential. Care should be taken not to place the pin on the PAP or more than 1 1/2 inches away from the PAP.

Very "Very" Dry Lanes

SKID FLIP DRILL - Of all the conditions we face concerning a house shot, no condition is more frustrating than being on **a lane that has a dry front end and <u>also a dry back end.</u>**

Considering the environment you are trying to conquer. You have to understand there is oil on the pattern but it is **spotty**. Yes, it harms more than it helps because it will make the ball jerk, or catch in places as it travels to the back end.

You will want to use a ball that has **a stable roll**. Also, a ball that will give you extreme length down the floor **without the snap**, or very violent flip at the back end like the **"FLIP DRILLED" layout will give you depicted in illustration #18. The flip drill will be quite unstable at the backend.**

Remembering that a ball pinned on your PAP will be in a stable drill you will have to use your hand to change your axis rotation and tilt to get to the back end.

Using a ball that is pinned high and at least 4 ½ to 5 1/2 inches away from your PAP should make the ball stable enough to smooth roll to the back end. **Provided the Mass Bias is not posted in the strong position** to the right for right-handed bowlers or to the left for left-handed bowlers.

The following illustration would be **a general layout** for a **very, very dry** lane for which getting to the backend may be successful.

This is commonly known as the **"SKID - FLIP** DRILL" layout for **wet backends.** This dual-purpose layout again can be used when the pattern is **Dry to Wet** in the direction you are delivering the ball.

Try this layout **during buffed out conditions** and **when there is carry down**, especially if you should start encountering splits such as the 4/9, the 7/10 and the 5/7.

(Skid-Flip layout)

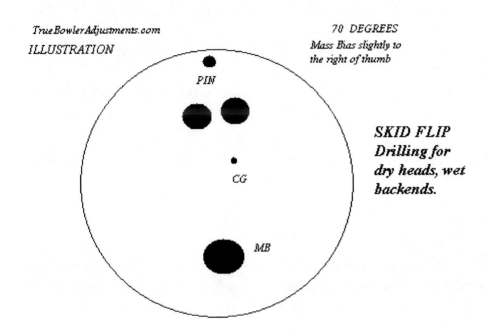

TrueBowlerAdjustments.com
ILLUSTRATION

70 DEGREES
Mass Bias slightly to
the right of thumb

PIN

CG

MB

SKID FLIP
Drilling for
dry heads, wet
backends.

Pin position for a very very dry shot. Depends on PAP
location and outer cover grit of 2000 to 4000. This
drill creates a stable roll to the pins. Can also be used
for high oil, buffed out backends, or any other Dry to
Wet condition.

This layout may **also** be useful for patterns that have very little oil in the
heads or front end, and the **back ends have been buffed out** to provide skid
or a hold spot prior to the ball entering the pins. (**This is not the same as
carry down**)

With experience, you will know when your ball is burning up on the front end
with no energy to finish on the back end as evident from consistent 10 pins.
(right handers) In this situation, you have to create more skid somehow on the
front end of your shots. **More skid often equates to better pin carry.**

Tournament Shots - For obvious reasons a tournament shot can take on many faces. However, one observation is that people generally will attack the lanes from the same positions. What to target is easy, you can loft a shot from 22/26 out to the 15 board on a wet shot and firm hand release. You stand so you can roll the ball at the 17 board out to the 10 board on a dry shot, with slow hand release. You can stand so that you roll your ball over the 11 board out to the 9 board. Also, you can stand so that you can project your ball around the 5 board down to the 8 board and back into the pocket.

Now, answer this question if you will? What bowling balls are you using for each of these shots? What do the heads look like? Do you have a bowling ball with a stable drill? Can you get good revolutions on the ball? Have you learned how to play beside the track area, as well as on it? Can you adjust like tournament bowlers need to do? Are you capable of delivering at least two different release shots that will help you score? Do you have a coach with tournament shot experience that can help you succeed?

With each bowling experience comes a sense of accomplishment. **Even if you don't do well scoring wise during tournaments, the experience teaches you what you can change to be a better bowler the next time you face that tournament pattern.**

Bowling Ball Cover - Saving the best for last - Many Bowlers asked me how do I get the ball to hook in soooo much oil. I simply tell them I use 150 or 250 grit sand paper or pads (Scotchbrite) that I buy from Walgreens or Home Depot in the paint section. That is it. Nothing fancy. I am very slow. You are responsible for your bowling! You are responsible for trying things that will work for **YOU.** Today's modern pro shops sell **abralon pads**. You will observes bowlers everyday throwing bowling balls that just slide down the lanes laboring and laboring to get back to the pins and they have no ball surface contact. They paid all that money to use a ball that won't hook, and it's supposed too, no way!!!

Wrong, it will hook; just make the surface rough enough to create the friction you need for your game. **Also,** use **"the correct release"** for the condition. **There is no way to tell what grit surface is on the person's bowling ball next to you ... is there? Buying the abralon scuff pads from the pro shops will give you the best idea of what surface you have on your ball. Most pro shops have a ball maintenance plan you can use throughout the year.**

Coaching - What a coach watches out for as you practice:

Coaches watch several items to ensure you have an enjoyable, educational, and safe experience. Listed at the end of this heading are several observations. Use these as guides to address key points in practice.

Practice is the time to develop a routine that will allow you to go over your mental checklist prior to getting on the approach. That way you will not stand there checking every aspect of your shot while on the approach.

The longer you are on the approach the more stress is placed on your arms. The tension created takes away from your delivery. It is described as **making the bowler weaker and weaker at the line, the longer they stand there.** The ball begins to drop while you are standing there evaluating way too much. Cover your routine before positioning yourself on the approach. Apply any final adjustments, and then execute your shot with confidence.

When a coach is monitoring your practice sessions, they will be watching how you deliver and **release** the ball - **spinner, stroker, or end-over-end, cranker, full roller, or backup ball release.** It is very hard for a coach and especially a ball driller, to assist you **if they cannot interpret how you are releasing the ball onto the lanes in one of the above manners.**

Coaches will check your ball fit! This will make sure you are **not losing the ball in the downswing or at the bottom of your swing.** Coaches see if you are drifting as you deliver the ball, if your ball position is high or low, if you take a 4 or 5-step approach, if your speed to the foul line is slow, medium, or fast. A coach will watch **your ball reaction,** whether or not your ball travels over your target, **watch for eye dominance issues,** and if you have **good balance at the line** after your release.

Hopefully, the coach will give you a recommendation for bowling balls that are of your particular speed and performance abilities. Coaches often may have unorthodox methods for training such as spinning the ball in practice on the ball return rack, or tossing a football underhanded, and having you balance on your slide foot at the foul line and project the ball onto the lane. Some coaches will have you on one knee so that you can release the ball on the approach to see how the ball hooks. Some may have you use a coca cola bottle, holding the neck while placing the side of the bottle against your forearm. Each exercise is geared to give a true bowler, **a consistent release** with confidence, and the best tools for success on the lanes.

Confidence is the cornerstone for coaches. Teaching bowlers to have confidence propels many bowlers from mediocre beginner bowlers, to a force to be reckoned with on the lanes.

Repeating Shots – Everyone has their own formula. I will list factors you can try that will allow you to repeat shots. #1 - **Watch your ball position.** During play, bowlers have a tendency to get tired. This tiredness will sometimes **lower** your ball position, changing your reaction on the lane.

Most often, this will cause your shot to finish or hook sooner, chiefly because you become slower. Don't go slower when you lower the ball unless you have to, conversely, sometimes we will acknowledge that we are a little tired by getting on the approach, taking that deep relaxing breath in and out, however, we'll raise the ball **"too high"** trying to compensate.

This will reduce hook on the ball and cause it to skid longer on the lane. Often, leaving our dearest friend the 10 pin. **Ball position** (height of where you hold the ball in your stance) is **very important** when it comes to repeating shots. **When you are tired, check your ball position!!!**
Foot pressure - Each of us has our own balancing point or stance at the line.

A solution for those who teeter-totter before beginning their approach: Stabilize yourself as the coaches have instructed you, then go one step further by knowing when to place your weight **on your front foot, or your back foot.**

Placing weight on your front foot and re-adjusting your body posture will often get you into the runners position just enough to give you consistent speed to the foul line.

Conversely, distributing your weight to your back foot will serve to slow your approach to the foul line **and balance you.** Just ensure you repeat this stance in your pre-shot talk to yourself and follow through in doing it. **Knowing your foot pressure will help you to repeat shots.**

Footsteps and the push away - I know that everyone has their own system for adjusting. Ironically, when you try what someone else suggested to you, and then mention it to someone else, they will often comment, "that's what I try to do!" **I call this identifying!** When you can identify with someone else about a particular move or **adjustment,** you know you are on the right track. Especially, if you can get your moves on the lanes confirmed by others. The push away is a point of fact. It is very important you consistently time your push away and your strong side foot together as you move towards the foul line in a four-step delivery.

It takes some practice with multiple steps; however, as long as the 1st of the last 4 steps and any combination of steps should be in unison with your push away or ball movement. The first step in a four-step routine should be the push away and your strong side foot moving together in harmony, like walking a tight rope your ball side foot will step over and in front of your slide foot to make room for the ball swing. This step and push away is the same length and cadence. Most professional bowlers **will simply roll the ball over into the swing from the non-ball or support hand** instead of using a push away to get the ball moving and into the swing.

Concerning timing, and the 5 step delivery, it is best to delay the ball movement until **after the second step** so that the ball swing back and the 3rd step coincide with each other. **Design your push away to go out and in-line with your target.**

Good timing in your push away will help you to repeat your shots.

200 + on most conditions - What is required to score 200+ on most conditions is just the ability to get the ball to the pocket without incurring impossible splits that you cannot convert or make on your spare shots.

You must tell yourself <u>to be close to the pocket</u> **for the best ball reaction.** I have noticed that the30 to 45-degree release with its low to high track pin mixing action is a good release as long as there are lots of revs at the backend.

Revolutions increase as the ball begins to slow down and read the lanes. This is excellent when combined with a surface that will get you good length on the ball. The ball cannot **"roll out"** on you! Nor can the ball be overthrown to the pocket skidding and hooking from too far from the outside **passed the front of the head pin**.

* Single Targeting (NOT RECOMMENDED) - **Knowing** where to move on the approach will often get more length out of the ball. **Knowing** where to move on the approach will bring the ball into the pins sooner.

Contrary to what is preferred by most coaches, bowlers often will employ the use of **a single target.** With a single target, there is **a huge amount of room for error.** Nevertheless, I will address single targeting **in general.** The majority of bowlers will look at a dot, or an arrow or some other mark on the lane.

To bring the ball **to the right side of the headpin** you can **move to your left** on the approach. If you are looking at a single target and **you want the ball to go left of the headpin,** you can **move to the right on the approach and throw at the same target.**

If you move up or back on the approach and wish to bring the ball to the right or left of the headpin, then your target has to be on the right or left side of you and **never** directly in front of you.

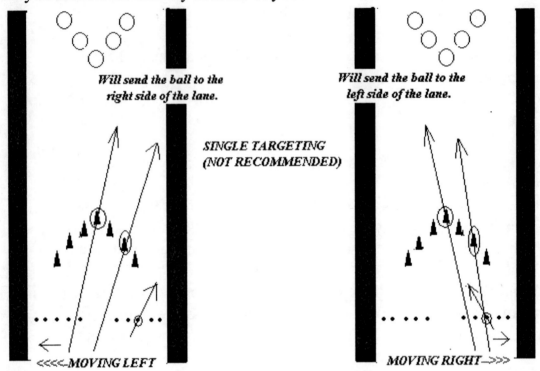

Will send the ball to the right side of the lane.

Will send the ball to the left side of the lane.

SINGLE TARGETING
(NOT RECOMMENDED)

<<<<—*MOVING LEFT*

MOVING RIGHT—>>>

Accomplished with your target to the left side, or to the right side of you. If you move up on the approach, you will send the shot more to the outside of the lane towards the gutters. If you move back on the approach and throw at a single target this will bring the ball more to the inside and closer to the middle of the lane. Remember to use your lead foot to point where you want to throw the ball. That is, if you choose to use **single targeting.**

STAYING IN THE POCKET

I thought long and hard about publishing how to get to the pocket and stay in the pocket. Every coach adopts what he or she knows best to suit the bowler's needs based on their style of play. I describe only one form of adjustment here however, trust that there are many, many more and through experience you will find what works for you.

What you can do **to stay in the pocket** is **figure out how to play the lanes during practice. FIRST,** stand where you normally like to play the lanes and throw a shot one foot in front of your normal target and read the balls reaction down lane. Remember keep your speed up as you deliver the ball. **SECOND,** stand where you normally like to play on the same lane and deliver the ball one foot beyond your normal spot to deliver the ball and again, read the balls reaction down lane. This will give you a good idea **if your ball hooks more the further** you deliver the ball out onto the lanes, **or if it skids longer down lane without reaction the further** you throw the ball out onto the lanes. YES, **both reactions need to be checked out during practice** so that you will know which way to adjust during the game. Once you decide which way to move to get you to the pocket you can almost be assure that if you have to deliver the ball out farther **it will skid more, or hook more** based on what you noticed during practice.

*** Note – The above text is **"why"** you **should not buy** a bowling ball that is **too heavy** for you to manipulate when it comes to delivering a well-placed shot onto the lanes in different spots. If this gives you an "ah hah" moment then now you have become **a Truebowler!**

Lanes that are **long oiled,** or have been **reversed buffed** will often provide **a hold spot** (skid) down lane for (**further ball travel**) allowing you to deliver the ball out further onto the lanes providing **more skid** to the pocket. The ball drilling may be one that is pinned above or below your fingers for **a stable roll** on the backend, or perhaps pinned near your PAP.

Lanes that are **short oiled,** or buffed out very short, **will hook more** as you move forward, and project the ball out farther onto the lanes. On **short oiled** lanes, the oil will be heavier back towards the foul line **allowing you to set the ball down earlier for increased length on the lanes.** However, this short oiled lane may cause your ball to read too soon, requiring you to employ a **flip drilled** layout, or a **skid-flip layout.**

The **skid-flip drilled** ball can be pinned high above your fingers. The **flip drilled** ball will be pinned up and out closer to your **VAL** (vertical axis line) causing the ball to go long however it will react very violently on the backend. Lastly, a reverse pattern/short pattern **is dry in the middle.** When reverse patterns exist or **you think it exist**, a bowler may move more to the **outside boards** of the lanes hopefully and fine oil there. **Summary:** Throw **three good shots** in practice. 1st Shot – 1 Foot before your target, 2nd Shot – At your target, 3rd Shot – 1 Foot beyond your normal target and read the balls reaction each time. This way you will know what to do should the lanes start to dry out.

When nothing seems to work, **one of the biggest problems with bowlers is just having one way to deliver the ball.** Getting to the head pin in good shape is the highest priority. Delivering just an end-over-end shot will work. However, when it is not working, simply *<u>switching to a spinning release as described on page 52, may give the ball the reaction you need to score.</u>*

Having two methods to deliver the ball is a beautiful thing. If your opponent is scoring with and end-over-end delivery … **take the hint.** This often is the simplest adjustment to do. **As with all adjustments, <u>keep it under your hat,</u> so your competition doesn't get the edge on you. Things like this are NOT shared among teammates or even friends at times so don't feel bad if someone just tells you to land the ball a little earlier, or to pitch the ball out a little farther, just try it. They may have a better read than you do. However, <u>good guidance is always appreciated without divulging your secrets.</u>**

Why is the PAP important ??? When considering the ball path to the pocket, your **PIN PLACEMENT** can be adjusted, or fine-tuned to the pocket by finding your PAP. Once found you can experiment with moving the **mass bias** to the **right** to increase the **revs** on the front end of ball travel or move the mass bias to the **left** to decrease the revs on the front end. Likewise, once you find your PAP, you can **extend your break point** down lane, by **moving the pin farther up,** or provide arc or snap to the breakpoint by moving the **pin to the right.** To get and **earlier roll** you can **move the pin down** a bit. <u>This is based on the release you are using with that ball.</u>

Game plan for dry lanes
What many good bowlers forget during play is that you need to back off on squeezing or revving the ball when the lanes are dry. *(Trying to throw or "spin" the ball harder defeats the issue.)* Most of the time, in an effort to increase ball speed down the lanes, **bowlers hit the ball more with their fingertips.** *The ball will only burn up on the front end.* **Especially, if your layout is an early rev layout.**

Conversely, you truly need to firm up, and rev up when the lanes are wet. (Also, having oil on your ball when it returns to you, does not tell you how long the oil pattern is. Only you will know if the ball is just not coming back to the pins. This can be figured out during practice. For dryer lanes, lift the ball off the finger joints.

With the 45 degree (1 o'clock release) and the spinning release there is **little surface contact with the lane** through the heads and a bowler is almost always assured of getting to the pocket on most conditions were there is some head to mid lane oil.

The unique aspect of the spinning release is that the release occurs when the fingers are lengthwise and exits the bowling ball in the 3 o'clock position well after the thumb has cleared, and the hand has rotated around to the side of the ball. **Having a flip drilled ball** alleviates some of the headache of the ball not finishing at the backend, **especially if you are slow to the line.**

Delivering the ball off the finger joints in an effort to "roll the ball" further down lane. Also, using the pad of the ring finger to spin the ball initially will help to get more length on the ball.

When spinning the ball, the release point is just posterior to the slide foot heel. At this point, the bowling ball finger holes are in a stacked position at the back of the ball in reference to the lane. The thumbhole is forward and pointing down lane.

When viewed from the side of the bowler the tilt of the bowlers hand or fingers in the ball will change the frictional aspect of the ball and increase its hooking action. As the thumb rotates back, it goes from being parallel with the fingers and the lane, to being perpendicular, or straight up and down to the lane. Zero degrees, or to 90-degrees, where the thumbhole is directly above the fingers, or in a 12 o'clock position.

How many adjustments are enough? If you must have a straight answer, it would be no less than 2 adjustments to correct the problem! If you make 2 adjustments that is fine, or even 3 adjustments its okay. Try not to make any big moves. The solution for over adjustment is simply taking one adjustment away until you are comfortable. **Reminder**….Point your slide foot heel and toe, in the direction you want to go! **Always remember to tell yourself to just throw a good shot once you are on the approach.**

You cannot make any adjustments off bad releases. At least 3 adjustments will give you a definite feel if you are adjusting in the right direction. **That direction is simply, did the shot get better or worst? Did it go longer or come in high on the headpin?**

Instead of being disappointed and bringing drama into the situation **simply "read" your ball reaction. Know how the ball reacted, even if there was no reaction at all.**

Courage to try something different equates to learned and gained experience. Prior experience, from past mistakes, makes and molds excellent competitive and non-competitive bowlers who continue to grow and share that knowledge with the next *generation.*

When a Truebowler who has bowled for years with a 150 average gets **the right information for making adjustments,** and the right bowling ball in their hands that match their delivery speed; how many adjustments to make, becomes a matter of whether or not the **ball is going too long or too short.** Most bowlers will adjust by **changing bowling balls first.** You will see this again and again. They are hoping that the cover and the layout of the next ball will make the difference and that they will match up quickly.
 Second to that, they will then modify the shot with a body adjustment once the approximate distance to the pocket is acquired. If they are really smart, they will recognize **what release they are delivering** and try changing it, or being more consistent with it. **Summary:** Make 2 or 3 small adjustments you can always take one away. Even if it is just a ball change with better surface.

Quick Reference Adjustments: Know where you are laying the ball down as it enters the heads; did you lay down just over the foul line, at 1 foot or out to 2 feet or are you lofting as much as out to the first set of dots 3 feet away onto the lane? **Knowing that spot on the lanes where the ball lands is paramount.** It is critical nowadays, especially with dry heads.
To combat dry heads the adage is to loft over them, use a low friction ball, or a particle-pearlized ball, or use **a spinning release.**

<u>Using Your Eyes</u>
 7 Pin leaves – Right handers, the ball is coming in too high. You are asking the two pin often to take out the 4 and the 7 pin and it will often only get one of them. Move right one board. Set ball down earlier, throw straighter to the break point with speed. Throwing straighter should be translated to a more end-over-end release or flatter wrist position. *Repeat your previous delivery* **with good speed using more skid.** *More skid is needed by all bowlers to delay hooking before the break point. Often employing **more pressure to the ring finger** during release is all that may be required to spin the ball out of the heads further down lane. Spinning out of dry heads may give a lengthier shot, creating more skid and a stronger backend, depending on the lane condition during play.* **A reminder also, that a 3 board move on the approach will often equate to a 2 board change at the pins.**

Be mindful that a 7 pin leave is also a sign of a very weak ball. This is a ball that barely took out the 5 pin. Use your eyes to determine whether the ball is very weak, 7 pin and 5 pin almost left standing; or if the ball generated the 4 pin and 7pin leave a strong ball reaction, and only the 7 pin remained standing.

USING YOUR EYES

10 Pin leaves –- Ball surface and lane contact on the backend as the ball enters the pocket is crucial. When the ball is still <u>skidding</u> and <u>hooking,</u> it often has very little surface contact. As long as it is skidding and hooking, "it basically does you no good." The ball often times needs to grab the lane at the backend, rev up, and get into a "roll" close enough to the pocket to carry strikes.

If it arrives on the side of the head pin this often leaves the ten pin. The ball needs to not just "hit" into the headpin or pocket, but to literally be <u>"rolling"</u> quite flatly into the "front portion" of the head pin to STRING STRIKES, by kicking out the 5 pin. This is something <u>your eyes</u> need to figure out!

Two situations exist when leaving ten pins normally. You are either rolling out too far away from the head pin(ball never makes it back to the front potion of the head pin and hits weak), or you are over throwing the pocket (passing by the head pin, skidding and hooking still). Both cases hitting the headpin too much on the side of the pin without a good "roll" on the ball.

Are you rolling out too far from the head pin? (hitting the pocket with a weak ball) or, <u>"can you see"</u> you are over throwing the headpin (too fast) and the bowling ball is going too long? Also, leaving 10 pins!!!!!

Sometimes you can get the ball to "roll" flatter from an angle, sometimes from straight on through the back of the pin deck, depending on the oil pattern. When leaving 10 pins, <u>your eyes</u> need to decipher what is happening at the headpin and what is happening with the bowling ball as it is traveling through the pins and falls off the back of the pin deck.

Think to yourself, as long as the ball is "skidding"…. And "hooking" it is not doing you a damned bit of good at all…(because it has very little surface contact and can be deflected) HOWEVER, when your ball gets into that back end "roll," that's when the ball means to take care of some serious business. Even the sound of the strike is totally different !!!

As mentioned before the ball needs to "roll" through the pins … to the left (strong ball) …to roll straight back through the pin deck (a sweet roll) …or it will roll back and to the right (weaker roll) …with a chance of carrying, but more of a chance of leaving ringing or solid 10 pins…often.

To hit harder or <u>to see</u> your ball <u>roll</u> sooner, you may have to lower your ball position if you can, and reduce your axis rotation as described on page 9 and 10. Somewhere between 45 degrees and zero degrees until you find the hit that carries for you. This position will often place your hand in a position to come more up the back of the ball (end-over-end, or forward rolling).

Practice, so you can release the ball just a little sooner and a little lower to the lane in more oil if need to increase the skid on your ball (spinning release). Ensure you apply pressure with your ring finger and middle finger pads while keeping your speed up. You can also step back just 3 to 6 inches. This will close your angle to the pocket just a bit (single targeting). This will bring the ball in sooner allowing better carry.

To kick out the 10 pin, often **you may have to** move your target further down lane at least 6" to 1 foot if you are in heavy oil (**Avoiding the head oil for longer patterns**). Moving your feet up on the approach helps to keep things normal, like your 40-foot house shot, as long as you **do not slow down** or loose sight of your targets. If your ball is rolling out before reaching the head pin, you can try using a little ball tilt and spin to clear the heads.

In addition, using a flatter or more stable wrist position will help, **along with reducing your revs sometimes** for an earlier **roll** to the pins. Reducing revs, **may** provide more traction or friction to kick out the 5 pin. Again, if the ball is skidding and hooking it has only a little traction and may deflect. Reducing revs can be as simple as breaking your wrist down, yet delivering the ball the same speed down lane.

"Roll" into the front potion of the head pin so you can string strikes!" You literally need **<u>to see</u>** if the bowling ball rolls to the <u>left</u>, <u>straight back</u>, or deflects <u>to the right</u> (weak ball for a right-handed bowler). If you cannot see this action of the ball through the pins, you need to **<u>work with a coach or someone trained</u>** to help you achieve this level of insight. Having the ability "to **see**" how the ball travels, can allow you to predict the way the ball may drive through the pins on the next shot. **This skill** is a jewel that "the best in bowling" have learned to master.

When the ball is coming in too high (or rolling too early) you will often be asking **the two pin** to come off the wall and take out the 4 pin and the 7 pin for total pin carry. **Often, it will only get one or the other of these two pins.**

Also, if the ball is coming in too weak you will have to <u>see with your eyes</u> that the ball deflects two much off of the head pin and covers two much of the <u>three pin</u> forcing it straight back. This movement of the ball going straight back often deflects the 6 pin to the wall, out and around the 10 pin. <u>Your eyes</u> need to literally **"see"** this happening so you will have a greater chance at **adjusting** to ten pin leaves.

Make the ball "roll" into the head pin by moving up. Throw straighter to the pins. Lower your revolutions, (breaking your wrist position down from cupping the ball). Loft the ball. Spin the ball out of the heads. Change your ball to a rougher ball surface or one that delays the skid. Use the hook and roll action of the ball to get you closer to the head pin. Increase your speed through your steps (faster tempo), or increase your speed by increasing your swing speed.

Conversely, your eyes will need **to see** when you are over throwing the head pin and hitting it on the side. In this case, you must find a way to reverse some items mentioned above so that you will cause the ball to skid less, hook less, **and roll into the pins a lot sooner.**

Also - If you move far to the "inside" of the lane – <u>change your end-over-end to a spinning release</u>. This may help the ball to clear the heads, and finish with a better roll on the backend. You have to get your ball to find good friction on the back end of the lane to carry consistently. Match up!

Preparing the cover of the bowling ball with a certain grit surface <u>is very important</u>. This will often allow you to clear the front end with easy while maintain a surface with the potential for consistent striking power.

"<u>Lastly, never be too far away from the pocket</u>." Giving yourself room to throw the ball out to the right or left a little more, often makes the ball <u>roll out</u> too far from the pocket which may not allow the ball to get back to the "front portion" of the head pin. The bowling ball hits more on the side potion of the headpin, <u>often results in deflecting the ball</u>. Especially if there is carry down. Many bowlers call this side potion of the headpin "the pocket." Watch the ball to make sure it is not tilted and skidding

into the pins, <u>instead</u> the bowling ball should be <u>rolling and revving up</u> as it finds its way to the "front potion" of the head pin *(while the pin in the ball is still up.)* <u>Moving up</u> will catch the pin in the up position to carry the 10 pin. It is a matter of distance to carry strikes most of the time.

Often I tell bowlers, <u>find your "40 FOOT" house shot.</u>

This way, <u>where you stand</u> can help you focus in on the breakpoint down lane.

Only when you know the backend is dry, will you attempt to come in from the outside. Perhaps that is why most bowlers have a good game in the beginning, and during the last game of play. Regardless, <u>you have to watch closely and see</u> how the ball is moving on the backend, to truly know if you have too much or too little friction.

Scuffing the surface of the ball for more friction prior to the start of league or tournament play will help also. **Also, you have the option of stepping up 3 to 6 inches and moving left just a board or two, to get closer to the headpin. (this may be the best option to kick out ten pin.)** Please note that *the pattern you are bowling on determines **how far left** you can move along* *with **what release you are using.*** Very few times will you be able to move left before the ball squirts through the carry down on you. Often times leaving the (1,2,4,10 split), so be careful making big moves to the left.

"Some items have been repeated in prior paragraphs adjusting both for a ball going to long or coming up too short, or for the ball going Brooklyn, because people deliver the ball differently. The overall thought is to try something different for your game. You can't just keep throwing the same shot; you will often get the same results or something worst." Learn how to adjust for your game! Learn how to string strikes for your game!"

Quick Lane Reading Prior to Play - <u>PRACTICE SHOTS</u>

Lane reading - How is the middle oiled?

(<u>Dry</u>, <u>House Shot</u>, or <u>Very Wet.</u>)

<u>*YOU NEED TO REMEMBER HOW THE MIDDLE IS OILED WHEN*</u>
<u>*GOING AFTER SPARES AND STRIKES THROUGHOUT THE GAME.*</u>

1. How is the shot to the left at 7 pin?
  - Dry hooks into the left gutter - <u>Middle is DRY!</u>
  - House Shot dead on, no adjustments.
  - Very Wet - missed 7 pin on right side, ball skidded off the back of
    pin deck - <u>Middle is Very Wet!</u>

2. How is the shot to the right at the 10 pin?
  - Dry hooking and misses 10 pin the left ball rolls off the back of pin
    deck - <u>Middle is DRY!</u>
  - House Shot dead on, no adjustments.
  - Very Wet, miss 10 pin to the right, skids into the right channel
    -<u>Middle is Very Wet!</u>

3. Is the TRACK SHOT playable?
  - Very Dry, hooks back to the 2 pin or goes Brooklyn.
  - House shot, change to weaker ball when starts to hook.
  - Very Wet, very little hook. <u>Scuff ball.</u>

TOURNAMENT SHOTS - Conditions may start out wet on the track or second arrow area. (Depending on how many players are in the tournament and whether it is a two, three or four game format. Lane transition will often display <u>carry down in front of the three pin</u> after a half game or full game of play. What type of **release** you are using is very important. Having watched hundreds of amateur and professional matches often the differences boils down to **who is repeating their release** and **who is using the "wrong" release** for the shot.

Concurrently, you **may** need to have a lot of hand in the ball to get it to the backend and turn. **Try the end-over-end release in practice at first to see if this gets you to the pocket. Then try your spinning release to see if you have enough recovery at the backend.**

Bowling Ball Arsenal – You should work to have at least 4 bowling balls in your arsenal and as much as 6 at times depending on your skill level and release you are using. Placing the highest hooking ball in the top left corner of your **four ball** or **six ball** carrier simplifies the ball selection as your game progresses. Pinning the ball across the palm and up will often cater to those that spin the ball at release. **There is nothing wrong with having three balls that you spin, and three balls that you end-over-end with different covers and different cores as long as "you know your equipment!"**

The illustration at the bottom of this page is an example of how you may want to set up your bowling ball arsenal. It favors the end-over-end bowler. The drillings depicted are not to scale. Yet, you can see that the hook and set and the flip drilled bowling balls are pinned closer to the PAP and the Vertical Axis Line or VAL to allow the ball to flip at the end of ball travel down lane. Bowlers who work the inside of the ball at release excel once they get the layouts to match their preferred patterns and lane length of play. Now imagine 6 layouts and you can end-over-end the ball or spin the ball onto the lanes for 12 different reactions. This, combined with cupping the hand and releasing from the 6o'clock, 5o'clock and 3o'clock release positions can make you an impressive juggernaut on the lanes.

Ball Arsenal Setup:

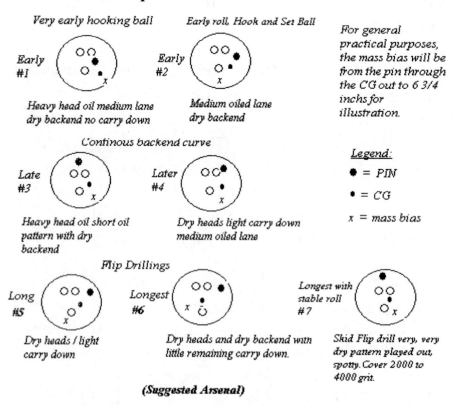

(Suggested Arsenal)

Each ball in your **arsenal** should subsequently go longer and not be hindered by the dry front ends. As you continue through your arsenal you will reach for bowling balls that go longer, and will read the lanes later.

These bowling balls will be able to often bite through the oil **carry down** from the front of the lanes (the heads) and flip on the backend through **the *carry down* where oil has deposited in front of the 3 pin and 6 pin.** This condition will cause the ball to slide past the headpin if you do not have the **proper layout** or adequate **revolutions** on the ball and **ball surface preparation** or **proper release** to get you out of the heads and back to the pocket.

Anticipate, when there are a lot of bowlers, that the condition in the heads will dry out eventually possibly requiring you to make another ball change, or going back to your original layout, but with a ball that has a higher grit surface (i.e. 2000, or 4000).

Use a cover that will get you out of the heads without loosing a great deal of ball reaction. Secondly, check your speed to the pins and do you need a ball that is continuous to the pocket or one that needs to **"flip"** into the pocket at the last minute of ball travel.   Layout **#3 and Layout #6 are both skid flip bowling balls.** Ball #3 is for **dry front ends with reversed buff.** Ball #6 is for **dry front ends and backends that may exhibit carry down.** For lanes that are just plain dry, **PURCHASING A SCOUT** reactive bowling ball by Columbia is my strongest recommendation, **complimented by a stable layout.** Some low reactive balls may have a puck inside them.

SPECIAL NOTE TO BOWLERS WHO PLAY THE SECOND ARROW OR TRACK SHOT

*** Learn to play either **two boards to the left or two boards to the right of the second arrow.**   The second arrow or 10 board is where everyone likes to play. This area gets a melt down of sorts. Second arrow is often very dry and will make the ball hook a lot.

You **"can" play** the second arrow; never think that you cannot play there. Play the second arrow only if you can get the ball to roll into the pocket. Use a lower friction ball to help get you down the lane if you need to later in the game.

BALL CHOICE SOLUTIONS WITH PIN AND MASS BIAS "SUGGESTED"

Dry Lane - Hooks into the left gutter / Track shot hooks to 2 pin/ Brooklyn / Hooks and misses to the left of 10 pin.

SHOT SOLUTION - Low Friction ball, move pin left from PAP, low core weight, Particle Ball, polished 2000 to 4000 grit finish. Also, move pin up and towards Vertical Axis Line with label drill. Move mass bias to the left side of the ball to delay revs.

Medium Lane --House Shot - Track shot, check to see if track is worn/dry. **SHOT SOLUTION - PAP is key, match cover and core. Find a coach. Use a higher pinned ball <u>if you are slow</u> in your delivery. Use a low pinned ball <u>if you are fast</u> in your delivery. Try not to be more than (3 3/8") from your PAP for max flare and backend response.**

<u>Wet Lane</u> --- **Skids to the right of 7 pin, skid off the back of the pin deck / skids into the gutter on the right side into the channel / Track area has very little recovery back to the head pin (carry down) this identifies oily central and backends also.**

SHOT SOLUTION - Freshly sand ball from 60 to 250 grit abrasion / Track Shots to the pocket, get low weight core, flip drilled ball or spare ball, or use large core ball for spare shots if you like(slow players). Large core balls FLIP DRILL high pinned, may be more effective on longer patterns. Especially when delivered straight to the pocket.

General targets for wet and dry shots - There are countless targets you can use to attempt shots. What is most needed by a Truebowler is **to line up two points on the lane** to consistently read your ball's reaction. **Good timing is always a key factor.** If you have the four Brunswick markers or range finders at the back of the lane you can use them.

If you are looking close, at arrows, or dots, you can use the pin position down lane as a secondary target. For example: Using the 3rd arrow and the 6 pin would be aligning the 15 board and the 10 board for a two targets or points on the lane.

Just practice and find an area or **set of targets** that may work for you. **Your game plan** should be to recognize what pin fell last, or was left standing. Then make the adjustment, especially if you know you delivered a good shot. For example, if you leave the 10 pin the ball needs to finish closer to the pocket. By keeping your same target and stepping back 3 to 6 inches you change the angle to the pins and bring the ball in sooner.

Also, if you move left one board and up 3 to 6 inches and your target left one board you will be closer to the headpin for better carry. Always **work on your game plan** and know what you are going to do should your reaction change.

HOW TO STAY ON LINE TO THE POCKET

TrueBowler's Game Plan – Generally a bowler's game plan is to throw straight or end-over-end in fresh oil and then move to the middle as play continues. Eventually the bowler may begin to swing the ball (changing to a spinning release) to the outside, a little or a lot, depending on their talent and skill.

The bowler may reach their limit of moves to the inside of the lane and move back to the outside edge of the lane where they began playing at first.

The bowler may keep moving to the outside until that limit has been reached also. **The decision to move to the left first or to the right is totally the decision of the bowler.**

Your game plan: First, <u>find a spot to deliver the ball</u> on the lane, where the ball gets to the pocket consistently. **Select the release you are going to use, and deliver good shots.** If needed, **change your release. Most house shots are 39 to 40 feet! You have to <u>find your 40-foot starting spot.</u>**

*** When you are **in high oil** at the front end of the lanes you will know this because often **you cannot spin the ball out to the right or to the left.** What immediately happens is, either the ball goes in the channel or it goes down lane and never recovers back to the headpin.

If the ball does not recover down lane, we often say the ball hits the **OOB** or "Out of Bounds" area. It just skids down the lanes only taking out one to three pins, or it creates a split with a spinning release, pretty much like landing in carry down oil.

Most bowlers will immediately change their delivery to an End-over-End release to stay on the lanes and keep the ball in play. Others will try moving left until they can keep the ball in play and **adjust** as they see fit.

Next, pick out the **next nine spots you will be using** based on the TrueBowler method as follows: When you move to the left, make your **move back 6 inches to 1 foot, first** and **then to your left by two boards.** *Keep your speed up. Do not spin the ball out of your hand unless that is the release you need. Likewise, do not throw the ball end-over-end if you were* *spinning it well at release. As you move more to the middle, you will find spinning the ball out of the front end may make it finish on the backend.*

The end-over-end may roll out more on the backend as you move to the middle of the lane and beyond.

Adjust your target on the lane by the same distance that you stepped back. When you notice it is time to move again, move back 6" to 1 foot again, and two additional boards to the left, **once again remembering to keep your speed up.**

You should be able to **use your initial target as a second reference spot for delivering the ball along the same line** to the pocket.

*** From your original starting spot on the approach move your feet left **5 boards and your target left 3 boards** and make the same moves again along a **new line** to the pocket. Remember a **(new line)** to the pocket but you are often going to come back through the **same break point** at the backend! This comes in handy when you have started out throwing the ball straight up the lane to get into the pocket.

Whereas you only need to step back 6" for a new lay down spot on a straight line giving you 3 positions to use. Moving to your left, back 6" and 2 boards left as described above will give you **9 spots** to deliver your bowling ball to, along 3 separate lines to the pocket.

Always remember if you move by adjusting **back** or **up** with your feet, you will need to move your first target the same amount of distance, **back** towards you or **up** away from you, to keep that same breakpoint **without slowing down**. Maintain that **40-foot** mentality as much as possible! Or whatever the length of the oil pattern is that day.

Hopefully, each spot will take 6 or 7 deliveries. *Remember, do not waste strikes in practice!* **Once you find your line to the pocket, practice is over! If not, you will just begin to deplete more oil away from your sweet spot.**

1st **Practice your corner pin spares so you know where to stand for them.**

***Then practice your strike shots so you will have that muscle memory for your first ball of the game.

*** Back 6 inches or 1 foot, then move left 2 boards and throw the same line back to the pocket.

Missing the front-end target. Most bowlers do not think about front-end targets, and what factors come into play when they miss them by one or two boards. Practically speaking, a miss of two boards on the front-end target often means a miss on the backend from 5 to 10 boards, especially on a house shot. It is even worse if you are **opposite eye dominant!**

Missing the back end target by one or two boards is often the difference of getting a strike or leaving a 10 pin or worse, getting a split. Always have two targets to keep you on track and cross both of them. **Confirm this by having good balance at the line so that you can "post your shot" (have good balance at the line after delivering the ball) and watch your ball travel.**

A way to stay on line to your target is to use the heel and toe of your slide foot. Should you miss your target to the inside of the lane, adjust your heel more to the outside or to the non-ball side and point your toe towards the targets you intend to hit on the lanes.

Many bowlers, regardless of where their targets are will inadvertently point their slide foot down lane instead of on angle, "at their targets." Next time, try targeting from your heel through the toe of your slide foot to your targets. The goal is to have both feet going in the same direction.

With any adjustment, **keep your speed up** to avoid unintentionally adding an adjustment. Slowing down will make the ball roll earlier. Good for kicking out ten pins sometimes, however you must practice this speed change to see if you can get a better carry by slowing down.

Remember, when you miss your target by a little bit when delivering on the approach end of the lane, the ball can miss as much as 5 to 6 boards on the backend depending on your speed. So moving a little on the approach may be your best bet to not end up with terrible leaves until you get lined up.

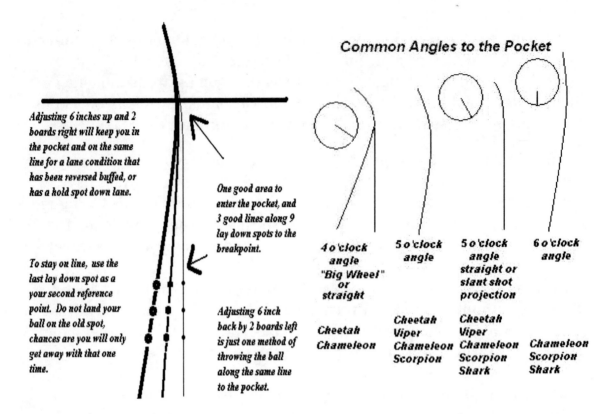

Common Angles to the Pocket

Adjusting 6 inches up and 2 boards right will keep you in the pocket and on the same line for a lane condition that has been reversed buffed, or has a hold spot down lane.

One good area to enter the pocket, and 3 good lines along 9 lay down spots to the breakpoint.

To stay on line, use the last lay down spot as a your second reference point. Do not land your ball on the old spot, chances are you will only get away with that one time.

Adjusting 6 inch back by 2 boards left is just one method of throwing the ball along the same line to the pocket.

4 o'clock angle "Big Wheel" or straight	5 o'clock angle	5 o'clock angle straight or slant shot projection	6 o'clock angle
Cheetah Chameleon	Cheetah Viper Chameleon Scorpion	Cheetah Viper Chameleon Scorpion Shark	Chameleon Scorpion Shark

FINE TUNING YOUR GAME

#1 – Ball Fit

Ball fit, affects *ball swing*, which directly affects *ball travel*. If you swing your ball into the backswing and notice that you don't feel the middle finger, or that you don't feel the ring finger, or that the ball is too lose on your thumb, you have a problem. You cannot lose the ball at the in your swing or at the bottom of your swing, and think that it will make it to the pins consistently every time.

#2 – Eye Dominance

Over 18 years I have seen many bowlers who were always going Brooklyn on their shots and "not" getting to the head pin consistently. Part of the problem was bowling with one hand and seeing or targeting with the opposite eye.

Bowlers in this particular situation often will not have their forearms or the ball directed towards their targets. Often they will project the ball two to three board left of target(right handed bowlers) and must compensate by getting the ball further right of their shoulders, while keeping the elbow tucked into their side. This creates muscle memory.

10 pin misses to the left may often be of particular concern to a coach should they encounter an opposite eye dominance bowler. Standing behind the bowler to see approximate forearm projection angle can be helpful in trying to successfully deliver a strike ball every time or eliminating the once feared the 10 pin.

Remember, opposite eye dominant players may look as much as 3 boards off the path of the intended launch angle to their target or targets. Coaches have different ways to compensate for this misreading. Such as having the player look as much as 3 boards right of target. Some coaches will use the players drift on the approach to make up for missing a target. The known fact being that if a player's drift is 5 boards then subtracting an additional two boards from there starting point on the lane will make up for the missing of the target. Even in bowling math is some times very crucial to a bowler's success.

#3 – Lane Transition and Carry Down

With a watchful eye while delivering good shots, the advanced bowler (every bowler) should be aware of carry down and be prepared to "adjust!" Once you see indications of carry down, i.e. lightly hitting the head pin leaving the 2/4/5(bucket) or the 5 pin or the 5/7 pin split. Be prepared to make the ball "roll" earlier, no excuses. You have to create or make some kind of "drag" on the ball to get it to turn sooner and make the cut into the pocket!

#4 – Roll of the ball

Recognizing the "roll" of your ball is coming in too high, or rolling out too far away from the head pin allows you the edge over your competition. In most cases, as long as you have the equipment and physical skills to either "dry your ball out" when it is going "too long," or to make your ball "wet enough" to travel "further down lane" when needed. You have to find "adjustments" that are appropriate for you! *Does not matter whether you use body adjustments, adjust the bowling ball or change bowling balls, or whether you move to a different part of the lane, or use loft to change your roll.* You must find adjustments that you like to use and perfect them. Simply put, if standing at the first set of approach dots give you a drier shot or dries your ball out, then perhaps stepping back a foot and setting your ball down earlier with a spin release will make your ball wetter. How to make your shot wetter or drier simplifies things. It makes you think quicker under fire. It makes your realize quickly if you are matching up, or not.

#5 – Finishing High Flush

As a coach, I personally promote that it is better for bowler to finish high flush because I hate them complaining about leaving ten pins. Also, I know it will be a stronger ball to the 5 pin. In my opinion, most bowlers will finish high flush into the pocket often leaving the 4 pin or the 7 pin standing or both pins. When the pin comes in high on the head pin you are asking the 2 pin to come off the wall and take out the 4 pin and the 7 pin in which case it often will leave one of them standing.

Your job should be to recognize that the ball is indeed coming in too high and to adjust to make the ball "wetter" so that it will travel further down lane without overthrowing the headpin and conversely leaving the 10 pin on the opposite side! Keep in mind, a 3 board move on the approach often equates to a 2 board move of the ball on the backend at the pin deck.

#6 – Bowling Ball vs. the Billiards Theory according to TrueBowler!

(Have you ever played Pool before???) In every sport, you have to go in with a particular mindset or way of thinking to achieve your goals. There is a key, or strategy for victory in every sport. In bowling, I present to you the Billiards Theory for you to consider.

In billiards (or playing pool) you will often hit the ball at the bottom with a quick stroke of the pool stick to get the ball to draw back towards you. Most call this putting "english" or reverse spin on the ball. Often if you are near the pocket this will keep the first ball you hit from following the target ball into the pocket, thus loosing your turn to play. Attacking the ball at the bottom and making it spin back to you on the carpeted pool table is an awesome thing.

Even in golf you will see a golfer hit the ball down range and when the ball hits the ground it has so much back spin on it, that if the golfer over shot the hole the ball would spin back towards the hole reducing the amount of distance for a closer shot next time.

The mindset in bowling is to create a situation for the ball to travel through the pins, and not be deflected from its path to the back of the pin deck. In many ways, I am asking you to create a condition where the bowling ball comes off your hand, fingertips or finger joints that allows you the bowler, to spin it forward out of your hand.

This way, when the bowling ball hits the dry boards at the back of the lane and grabs on the 4-foot pin deck it, will "rev" up and push through the pins without deflecting.

In essence, we as bowlers need to try to create enough top spin, or forward spin on the ball that it "rolls" through the rack with a powerful hit. This hit leaves no doubt that the ball is being delivered correctly for that lane condition.

Getting behind this theory, and putting it in the forefront of your mind, will help you stay focused on your objective of being able to string strikes. Get the ball to rev up prior to making its "roll" phase into the pins.

CONCLUSION

The house shot or "bumper shot" is going to be difficult at first for anyone just starting to get the hang of reaction on the lanes. In truth, you may not get the ball to carry the entire game, but don't give up. ***There is*** *a place where* ***you can*** *throw the ball.* ***There is*** *place where* ***you can*** *stand on the approach.* ***There is*** *a speed with which you can walk and swing the ball.* ***There is*** *a particular surface, grit or polished* ***you can*** *put on your ball. There is* ***a layout or two*** *that you can use to finish at the pocket.* ***There is*** *a hand position* ***you can*** *put the ball in prior to release that will give you a proper reaction.* ***There is*** *an amount of loft* ***you can*** *use.* ***There is*** *a degree of finger pressure* ***you can*** *put on the ball.* ***There is*** *a balance at the foul line that is right for you and* ***there is*** *a target* ***you can*** *roll over to hit another target at the backend, repeating your shot time after time, if you focus,* ***if you learn to keep good timing.*** *This also applies to sport shots and PBA patterns.*

When someone says to you, "I just bowl for fun "- ***Leave them alone!*** *Let them enjoy themselves. In time, either they will "let" you help them, or they may even ask for help!*

The difference between a winner and someone who just wants to play the game. A winner ***"will remember"*** *what to do in game situations <u>during the entire event,</u>* ***especially during crucial must have performances.*** *Often a basic player* ***won't be able to remember*** *where to stand and what to target and may* ***often*** *be lost as to what to do in crucial situations such a shooting a 10pin, 7pin, a baby split, or getting that double wood spare when needed.*

<u>Knowing what to do</u> *is the mark of* **True Bowler**, *and* **a winner!**

Even if things do not work out the way you wanted them to. Strive to be a winner so you will **remember** *and* **know what to do!** *This is often the best stress reliever in any sport.* **Your average** *often dictates how much you* **"should"** *know about your bowling.* **Many bowlers fail to realize this!**

*When it comes to promoting the "***sport***" of bowling,* **professional and amateurs bowlers alike,** *take everything in the very first paragraph of this conclusion to heart. They apply it seemingly effortlessly on every delivery, even down to the pressure on the pads of their fingers. Often they work to match up to their bowling balls in a special way* **gaining knowledge** *and separating themselves from the field. Strive to separate yourself from the field!*

The sport shot, and other PBA shots are not normally a friend to those who have slow feet and slow ball revolutions. The inability of the bowler to repeat shots is greatly magnified. Use the known factors such as **how fast you deliver the ball** *and* **the length of the oil** *to your advantage. This way you will work to get the ball to grab the last 23 to 15 feet or dry boards to "***roll***" into the pocket and string strikes.*

Like most bowlers, we want an entry area into the lanes of 4 to 5 boards; however, with tougher patterns you may get only 2 to 3 boards of **area if you are lucky.** *The key thing for a True Bowler to understand is there has to be a "standard." The standard in bowling: Show others that you can* **"repeat shot after shot, no matter what lane conditions we place in front of you. Excel at spare shooting, and master the ability to adjust during the game!"**

The ability to dismiss drama, **<u>refocus, and adjust</u>** *is an admirable quality of a bowler regardless of your skill level. A True Bowler needs physical training to learn consistency,* **continuous** <u>*education*</u>*, to find the* **right equipment,** *and the* **mental toughness** *to overcome shortcomings on the lanes.*

Bowling is truly a sport of longevity whether you compete or not. To every bowler out there, I wish you the greatest of success! I hope I have helped you in some way, by providing **<u>a book that truly helps you to adjust.</u>** **That was my goal!** *Think of others that may need help. You know they can bowl.* **My book can help them to adjust, and bowl better!**

Be a True Bowler!